HENRY B

GEORGES

GUYNEMER

KNIGHT OF THE AIR

TRANSLATED FROM THE FRENCH
By LOUISE MORGAN SILL

WITH AN INTRODUCTION BY
THEODORE ROOSEVELT

MDCCCCXVIII

British Library Cataloguing-in-Publication Data
A catalogue record for this book is available from the
British Library

Introduction to the

World War One Centenary Series

The First World War was a global war centred in Europe that began on 28 July 1914 and lasted until 11 November 1918. More than nine million combatants were killed, a casualty rate exacerbated by the belligerents' technological and industrial sophistication – and tactical stalemate. It was one of the deadliest conflicts in history, paving the way for major political changes, including revolutions in many of the nations involved. The war drew in all the world's great economic powers, which were assembled in two opposing alliances: the Allies (based on the Triple Entente of the United Kingdom, France and the Russian Empire) and the Central Powers of Germany and Austria-Hungary. These alliances were both reorganised and expanded as more nations entered the war: Italy, Japan and the United States joined the Allies, and the Ottoman Empire and Bulgaria joined the Central Powers. Ultimately, more than 70 million military personnel were mobilised.

The war was triggered by the assassination of Archduke Franz Ferdinand of Austria, heir to the throne of Austria-Hungary, by a Yugoslav nationalist, Gavrilo Princip in Sarajevo, June 28th 1914. This set off a diplomatic crisis when Austria-Hungary delivered an ultimatum to Serbia, and international alliances were invoked. Within weeks, the major powers were at war and the conflict soon spread around the world. By the end of the war, four major imperial powers; the German, Russian, Austro-Hungarian and Ottoman empires— ceased to exist. The map of Europe was redrawn, with several independent nations restored or created. On peace, the League of Nations formed with the aim of preventing any repetition of such an appalling conflict, encouraging cooperation and communication between the newly autonomous nation states. This laudatory pursuit failed spectacularly with the advent of the Second World War however, with new European nationalism and the rise of fascism paving the way for the next global crisis.

This book is part of the World War One Centenary series; creating, collating and reprinting new and old works of poetry, fiction, autobiography and analysis. The series forms a commemorative tribute to mark the passing of one of the world's bloodiest wars, offering new perspectives on this tragic yet fascinating period of human history.

Amelia Carruthers

A Timeline of the Major Events of World War One in Europe

1914

28th June   Franz Ferdinand Assassinated at Sarajevo.

29th June   Austro-Hungary send despatch to Vienna accusing Serbian complicity in the killing.

5th July   Kaiser Wilhelm promises German support for Austria against Serbia.

20th July   Austria-Hungary sends troops to the Serbian frontier.

25th July   Serbia mobilises its troops, Russia sends troops to the Austrian frontier.

28th July   Austria-Hungary Declares war on Serbia.

29th July	Austrians bombard Belgrade and German patrols cross the French border. Britain warns it cannot remain neutral.
1st August	Germany declares war on Russia. Italy and Belgium announce neutrality. French mobilisation ordered.
3rd August	Germany declares war on France and invades Belgium (Schlieffen plan). Great Britain mobilises.
4th August	Britain declares war on Germany and Austria-Hungary (after ultimatum to stand down). US declares neutrality. Germany declares war on Belgium.
6th August	First British casualties with the HMS Amphion sunk by German mines in the North sea. 150 men dead.
7th August	First members of the BEF (British Expeditionary Force) arrive in France.

11th August	Start of enlisting for Kitchener's New Army 'Your King and Country Need You'.
20th August	Brussels is evacuated as German troops occupy the city.
23rd August	The BEF started its retreat from Mons. Germany invades France.
26th August	Russian army defeated at Tannenburg and Masurian Lakes. BEF suffers over 7000 casualties at the Battle of Le Cateau –forced to retreat.
6th September	Battle of the Marne starts; checks German advance, but at the cost of 13,000 British, 250,000 French and 250,000 German casualties.
19th October	First Battle of Ypres.
29th October	Turkey enters the war (on Germany's side).
22nd November	Trenches are now established along the entire Western Front.
8th December	Battle of the Falkland Islands.

1915

19th January	First Zeppelin raid on Britain (Great Yarmouth and Kings Lynn – killing 5).
18th February	Blockade of Great Britain by German U-boats begins. All vessels considered viable targets, including neutrals.
22nd April	Second Battle of Ypres begins. Widespread use of poison gas by Germany.
25th April	Allied troops land in Gallipoli.
2nd May	Austro-German offensive on Galicia begins.
7th May	The Lusitania is sunk by a German U-Boat – creating US/German diplomatic crisis.
23rd May	Italy declares war on Germany and Austria
31st May	First Zeppelin raid on London, killing 35 and shaking morale.

30th June	German troops use flamethrowers for the first time, against the British at Hooge, Ypres.
5th August	Germany captures Warsaw from the Russians.
21st August	Final British offensive in the Dardanelles (Scimitar Hill, Gallipoli). They lose, and suffer 5000 deaths.
25th September	Start of the Battle of Loos and Champagne. The British use gas for the first time, but the wind blows it over their own troops, resulting in 2632 casualties.
31st October	Steel helmets introduced on the British Front.
15th December	Sir Douglas Haig replaces Sir John French as Commander of the BEF.

1916

8th January

Allied evacuation of Helles marks the end of the Gallipoli campaign.

21st February

Start of the Battle of Verdun – German offensive against the Mort-Homme Ridge. The battle lasts 10 months and over a million men become casualties. (Finishes 18th December, the longest and costliest battle of the Western Front).

9th March

Germany declares war on Portugal. Six days later, Austria follows suit.

31st May

Battle of Jutland – lasts until 1st June. German High Seas Fleet is forced to retire despite having inflicted heavier losses on the Royal Navy (14 ships and 6,100 men). German fleet irreparably damaged.

4th June

Start of the Russian Brusilov Offensive on the Eastern front. Nearly cripples Austro-Hungary.

1st July	Start of the Battle of the Somme – 750,000 allied soldiers along a 25 mile front. Nearly 60,000 are dead or wounded on the first day.
14th July	Battle of Bazetin Ridge marks the end of the first Somme Offensive. The British break the German line but fail to deploy cavalry fast enough to take advantage. 9,000 men are lost.
23rd July	Battle of Pozières Ridge marks the second Somme Offensive, costs 17,000 allied casualties – the majority of whom are Australian. (ends 7th August).
10th August	End of the Brusilov Offensive.
9th September	The Battle of Ginchy. The British capture Ginchy – a post of vital strategic importance as it commands a view of the whole battlefield.
15th September	First use en masse of tanks at the Somme. The Battle of Flers-Courcelette signifies the start of the third stage of the Somme offensive.

13th November	Battle of Ancre. The fourth phase of the Somme Offensive is marked by the British capturing Beaumont Hamel and St. Pierre Division, taking nearly 4,000 prisoners.
12th December	Germany delivers Peace Note to Allies suggesting compromise.

1917

1st February

Germany's unrestricted submarine warfare campaign starts.

3rd February

US sever diplomatic relations with Germany as U-boats threaten US shipping. Intercepted messages reveal that Germany is provoking the Mexicans into war with the US.

21st February

The great German withdrawal begins. Serre, Miraumont, Petit Miraumont, Pys and Warlencourt are evacuated, falling back 25 miles to establish stronger positions on the Hindenburg Line.

15th March

Tsar Nicholas II abdicates as Moscow falls to Russian Revolutionaries. Demise of the Russian army frees German troops for the Western front.

6th April

USA declares war on Germany – troops mobilise immediately.

9th April	Battle of Arras. British successfully employ new tactics of creeping barrages, the 'graze fuse' and counter battery fire.
16th April	France launches an unsuccessful offensive on the Western Front. – Second Battle of Aisne begins as part of the 'Nivelle Offensive'. Losses are horrendous, triggering mutinies in the French Army.
7th June	The Battle of Messines Ridge. British succeed with few casualties, detonating 19 mines under German front lines – the explosions are reportedly heard from England.
13th June	Germans launch first major heavy bomber raid of London – kills and injures 594.
25th June	First US troops arrive in France.
31st July	Start of the Third Battle at Ypres – a 15 mile front in Flanders. Initial attacks are successful as the German forward trenches are lightly manned.

15th August	The Battle of Lens (Hill 70). – Canadians at the forefront , won a high vantage point, though loss of 9,200 men.
20th August	Third Battle of Verdun begins. French progress is marked by gaining lost territory in the earlier battles.
9th October	The third phase of the Ypres Offensive begins with British and French troops taking Poelcapelle. 25mm of rain falls in 48 hours and the battlefield turns into a quagmire.
12th October	British launch assault at Ypres Against the Passchendale Ridge. New Zealand and Australians take terrible casualties. Bogged down in mud and forced back to start lines.
24th October	Battle of Caporetto – Italian Army heavily defeated.
26th October	Second Battle of Passchendaele begins, 12,000 men lost and 300 yards gained (ends 10th November – 500,000 casualties,

140,000 deaths and 5 miles gained).

6th November	Britain launches major offensive on the Western Front.

6th November   Britain launches major offensive on the Western Front.

20th November   Victory for British tanks at Cambrai - The Royal flying Corps drop bombs at the same time on German anti-tank guns and strong points. Early example of the 'Blitzkrieg' tactics later used by Germany in World War Two.

5th December   Armistice between Germany and Russia signed.

1918

16th January	Riots in Vienna and Budapest with dissatisfaction at the war.
3rd March	Treaty of Brest-Litovsk signed between (Soviet) Russia and Germany.
21st March	Second Battle of the Somme marked by the German spring offensive, the 'Kaiserschlacht'. Germans attack along a 50 mile front south of Arras.
22nd March	Victory for Germany with operation Michael - Use of new 'Storm trooper' assault to smash through British positions west of St. Quentin, taking 16,000 prisoners.
23rd March	Greatest air battle of the war takes place over the Somme, with 70 aircraft involved.
5th April	The German Spring Offensive halts outside Amiens as British and Australian forces hold the Line. The second 1917 battle of

the Somme ends, as Germany calls off operation Michael.

9th April	Germany starts offensive in Flanders —Battle of the Lys (ends 29th April).
19th May	German air force launches largest raid on London, using 33 aircraft.
27th May	Operation Blucher – The Third German Spring Offensive attacks the French army along the Aisne River. French are forced back to the Marne, but hold the river with help from the Americans.
15th July	Second battle of the Marne started; final phase of German spring offensive. Start of the collapse of the German army with irreplaceable casualties.
8th August	Second Battle of Amiens – German resistance sporadic and thousands surrender.
27th September	British offensive on the Cambrai Front leads to the storming of the Hindenburg Line. Battle of St.

Quentin – British and U.S troops launch devastating offensives.

4th October	Germany asks the allies for an armistice (sent to Woodrow Wilson).
8th October	Allies advance along a 20 mile front from St. Quentin to Cambrai, driving the Germans back and capturing 10,000 troops.
29th October	Germany's navy mutinies (at Jade).
3rd November	Austria makes peace. German sailors mutiny at Kiel.
9th November	Kaiser Wilhelm abdicates and revolution breaks out in Berlin.
11th November	Germany signs the armistice with the allies – coming into effect at 11.00am (official end of WWI).

1919

10th January	Communist Revolt in Berlin (Battle of Berlin).
18th January	Paris Peace Conference Begins.
25th January	Principle of a League of Nations ratified.
6th May	Under conditions of the Peace conference, German colonies are annexed.
21st June	The surrendered German naval fleet at Scapa Flow was scuttled.
28th June	Treaty of Versailles signed.
19th July	Cenotaph unveiled in London.

By Amelia Carruthers

Air Warfare in the First World War

In 1903 the Wright brothers made the first recorded powered flight, achieving 12 seconds air time at Kittyhawk, Dare County, North Carolina, United States. In 1909, the first powered crossing of the English Channel was achieved by Louis Blèriot. Five years later, the First World War began.

Due to its still nascent technology, aviation was deemed of little use to the European armed services. One unknown British general commented that 'the airplane is useless for the purposes of war.' Likewise, the German General Ferdinand Foch is reported to have alleged that 'aviation is a good sport, but for the army it is useless.' These opinions reflected a widespread scepticism about aircraft, unsurprising given their delicate and undependable nature. Most aeroplanes in 1914 were constructed of hardwood or steel tubing, combined with linen fabric doped with flammable liquid to provide strength. They were incredibly fragile by later standards and frequently collapsed during flight, especially in combat situations.

As a result of these technical issues, when war erupted in July 1914, aircraft were used mainly for reconnaissance; feeding back information for artillery strikes, recording troop movements and taking detailed photographs of enemy positions. However, the diversity of uses, technological advances and sheer increase of numbers involved in air warfare during the period were astonishing. To illustrate, France had fewer than 140 aircraft at the outbreak of war, but by 1918 she had 4,500. However, France actually produced 68,000 aircraft during the war, with 52,000 destroyed in combat; a staggering loss rate of 77%. Aerial battles were extremely crude, but equally deadly – the pilots flew in tiny cockpits, making parachutes a rarity and death by fire commonplace. Many officers, especially the British, actually forbade the carrying of parachutes as it was feared they would lessen the fighting spirit of the men.

The typical British aircraft at the start of the war was the general purpose BE2X. It had a top speed of 72mph and was powered by a 90hp engine; it could fly for roughly three hours. By the end of the war, this had been replaced by planes such as the Sopwith Camel and the SE5a fighter, built for speed and manoeuvrability. The latter had a top speed of 138mph, now powered by a 200hp engine. The technological change which enabled these improvements was the 'pusher' layouts' replacement. Traditionally, propellers faced backwards, pushing the plane forwards – but the alternative design with a forward facing propeller (a 'tractor') provided far superior performance both in terms of speed and power. Another major advance was the replacement of the rotary engine. In this type of engine, where the crankshaft remained stationary whilst the pistons (attached to the propeller) rotated around it, there was an excellent power to weight ratio, but it lost out to the more powerful water cooled engines. By 1918, the Sopwith Camel remained the last major aircraft still using the older rotary technology.

Within the first months of the war, whilst still in the 'movement stage', the value of aerial reconnaissance was vindicated. On 22 August 1914, contradicting all other intelligence, one British Captain and his Lieutenant reported that General Alexander von Kluck's army was preparing to surround the BEF. This initiated a massive withdrawal towards Mons, saving about 100,000 lives. Similarly, at the First Battle of the Marne, General Joseph-Simon Gallieni was able to achieve a spectacular victory, using information provided by the French air force to attack the exposed flanks of the German army. But nowhere was the importance of aerial intelligence more forcibly asserted than at the Battle of Tannenberg on the Eastern Front. The Russian General, Alexander Samsonov ignored his own pilot's warnings, allowing almost all of his army to be captured or killed by the Germans. After the crushing defeat, Samsonov committed suicide whilst German Field Marshall Hindeburg stated 'without airmen, there would have been no Tannenburg.'

As aerial reconnaissance became more frequent and effective, new methods were developed to counter this threat. At first, infantry fired at planes from the ground, although this was largely ineffective due to ill-adapted guns. Yet quickly, airmen began directly attacking one another. Pilots and their observers attempted to shoot at the enemy using rifles and pistols; some threw bricks, grenades and ropes with grappling hooks attached. A more reliable solution was required. As early as 1912 the Vickers company had already produced an experimental airplane to be armed with a Maxim machine gun. Nicknamed the 'Destroyer', the EFB1 plane was powered via the old fashioned pusher layout, allowing the gunner to sit in front of the pilot, giving an uninterrupted field of vision. The nose was too heavy with the machine gun's weight though, and the plane crashed on its first flight. By 1914 many pilots took the initiative and experimented with machine guns themselves. The British pilot Louis Strange improvised a safety strap allowing the observer of his tractor driven Avro 504 to 'stand up and fire all round over top of plane and behind.' Similarly, on 5 October, 1914, a French pilot in a Voisin III pusher biplane became the first man of the war to shoot down another aircraft – his observer standing up to fire a Hotchkiss machine gun.

Only a few machine guns were small and reliable enough for use however, and the problem was not satisfactorily solved until Anton Fokker developed the 'interrupter gear' in 1915. This meant that a machine gun could be synchronised with the moving propeller blades – soon to produce the 'Fokker Scourge' for the allies. This development gave the Germans a strong advantage, not only strategically but in terms of morale. The Fokker, and its successor the *Eindecker* caused panic in the British parliament and press; also contributing to German successes at the Battle of Verdun as French reconnaissance failed to provide information on enemy positions. It took the allies an entire year to adapt the device to their own use.

These fighting aircraft were supported by the bombers; not directly involved in fights (if possible), but aimed at destroying the enemy's capacity to make war on the home front. Industrial units, power stations, shipyards and entire cities became targets; some of the most famous being Germany's Zeppelin raids on London – causing up to half a million pounds of damage with each vessel. At the start of the war, bomb aiming was crude in the extreme however. Bombs were simply dropped over the side of the aircraft when the pilot reached the vicinity of the target. Russia was the first to develop an airplane specifically for this purpose; the Murometz, a large four-engine airplane originally produced in 1913 as a passenger plane, was used successfully throughout the entire war. The Germans had the Gotha bomber plane, and the British had the Handley Page. Yet despite the strategic importance of these bomber planes, as the war continued it was the fighters who captured the public's imagination. Popular legends arose around the 'great aces' such as Manfred von Richthofen (the 'Red Baron'), Ernst Udet, and the French pilot Paul Rene Fonck. Governments were quick to trumpet the successes of their airmen for propaganda purposes, with the French and the Germans being the first countries to award the distinction of 'ace'.

This seemingly exotic and elegant war in the air was far removed from reality however. As noted, reconnaissance was the largest role of aircraft during the war, and the bravery of the pilots in fulfilling this dangerous and unglamorous work is seldom remarked. Newly recruited pilots were sent into the sky, often only with a few hours air training time (typically less than five), and as the war progressed it became unusual for new pilots to survive their first few weeks. The newer planes, often built more for manoeuvrability than stability were increasingly difficult to operate and if pilots were not shot down, bad weather, mechanical problems and simple pilot error could all intervene. Most died not in spectacular dogfights but after being shot from behind, unaware of their attackers.

Taken as a whole, air warfare did not play a fundamental strategic role in World War One, as it did in later conflicts – however bombers and fighters provided just as important a psychological weapon as they did a practical one. The main significance of World War One aviation was a rapid increase in technology and prestige, fostering a new found respect in the general public and military commanders for this hitherto unknown method of battle. The terrible capabilities of air warfare would be unleashed on a far greater scale in the next World War, with even more devastating consequences.

Amelia Carruthers

Memoirs, Diaries and Poems of World War One

In 1939, the writer Robert Graves was asked to write an article for the BBC's *Listener* magazine, explaining 'as a war poet of the last war, why so little poetry has so far been produced by this one.' From the very first weeks of fighting, the First World War inspired enormous amounts of poetry, factual analysis, autobiography and fiction - from all countries involved in the conflict. 2,225 English war poets have been counted, of whom 1808 were civilians. The 'total' nature of this war perhaps goes someway to explaining its enormous impact on the popular imagination. Even today, commemorations and the effects of a 'lost generation' are still being witnessed. It was a war fought for traditional, nationalistic values of the nineteenth century, propagated using twentieth century technological and industrial methods of killing. Memoirs, diaries and poems provide extraordinary insight into how the common soldier experienced everyday life in the trenches, and how the civilian population dealt with this loss.

Over two thousand published poets wrote about the war, yet only a small fraction are still known today. Many that were popular with contemporary readers are now obscure. The selection, which emerged as orthodox during the 1960s, tends to (understandably) emphasise the horror of war, suffering, tragedy and anger against those that wage war. This was not entirely the case however, as demonstrated in the early weeks of the war. British poets responded with an outpouring of patriotic literary production. Robert Bridges, Poet Laureate, contributed a poem *Wake Up England!* calling for 'Thou careless, awake! Thou peacemaker, fight! Stand, England, for honour, And God guard the Right!' He later wished the work to be suppressed though. Rudyard Kipling's *For All We Have and Are,* aroused the most comment however, with its references to the 'Hun at the gate... the crazed and driven foe.'

From Hemingway's *A Farewell to Arms,* to Remarque's *All Quiet on the Western Front,* to the poetry of Sassoon, Graves, and Brooke, there are numerous examples of acclaimed writing inspired by the Great War. One of the best known war poets is perhaps Wilfred Owen, killed in battle at the age of twenty-five. His poems written at the front achieved popular attention soon after the war's end, most famously including *Dulce Et Decorum Est, Anthem for Doomed Youth*, and *Strange Meeting.* In preparing for the publication of his collected poems, Owen explained 'This book is not about heroes. English poetry is not yet fit to speak of them. Nor is it about deeds, or lands, nor anything about glory, honour, might, majesty, dominion, or power, except War. Above all I am not concerned with Poetry. My subject is War, and the pity of War. The Poetry is in the pity.'

Dulce et Decorum Est, one of Owen's most famous poems, scathingly takes Horace's statement, 'Dulce et decorum est, pro patria mori', meaning 'It is sweet and proper to die for one's country' as its title. It chiefly describes the death of an anonymous soldier due to poison gas, vividly describing the suffering of the man, ending with a bitter attack on those who see glory in the death of others. Such themes were also widely utilised by authors unaccustomed with the literary canon - the common soldier noting down their experiences for their loved ones, and for posterity. Each unit in World War One was in fact required to keep a diary of its day-to-day activities, many portraying the anxiety and terror of the opening days of the war. Diaries from soldiers in the First Battalion South Wales Borderers (among others, recently released at the British National Archives) described the battles of the Marne and the Aisne, with one captain who said the scenes he witnesses were 'beyond description... poor fellows shot dead are lying in all directions... everywhere the same hard, grim pitiless sign of battle and war. I have had a belly full of it.'

Other, lighter aspects of everyday life including tugs of war, rugby matches and farewell dinners to mark the end of the fighting have also been documented, giving us a rare insight into what the First World War was like for the men on the front line. Letters were an incredibly important part of life as a soldier. Receiving and writing them helped keep them sane, and could take them away from the realities of trench life. Every week, an average of 12.5 million letters were sent to soldiers by family, friends, and partners. More formalised memoirs have also become a key way of understanding the conflict, from gas attacks, the fear of going over the top, methods of coping with death - as well as the jovial camaraderie which often grew up between the men. The first memoirs of combatants were published in 1922, not long after the armistice: *A Tank Driver's Experiences* by Arthur Jenkins and *Disenchantment* by Charles Edward Montague. These were shortly joined with *Good-Bye to All That* (1929) by Robert Graves, *A Subaltern's War* (1929) by Charles Edmund Carrington, and *Blasting and Bombardiering* (1937) byPercy Wyndham Lewis. Nurses also published memoirs of their wartime experiences, such as *A Diary without Dates* (1918) by Enid Bagnold, and *Forbidden Zone* (1929) by Mary Borden. Vera Brittain's *Testament of Youth* (first published 1933) has been acclaimed as a classic for its description of the impact of the war on the lives of women and the civilian population - extending into the post-war years.

Storm of Steel, written by Ernst Jünger, published in 1920 was one of the first personal accounts to be published - a graphic account of trench warfare, unusually glorifying the sacrifice encountered. The book has consequently been criticised for lionizing war, especially when compared with works such as Remarque's (albeit fictional) *All Quiet on the Western Front*. In the preface to the 1929 English edition, Jünger stated that; 'Time only strengthens my conviction that it was a good and strenuous life, and that the war, for all its destructiveness, was an incomparable schooling of the heart.' As is evident from this short introduction to the memoirs, diaries, letters and poems of the first world war

- it is an intensely complex field. Dependent on military rank, geographic position and placement, nationality and subjective experience and character, they take on a wide variety of forms and focuses. Such works give an amazing insight into the experiences of combatants and it is hoped the current reader is encouraged to find out more about this thoroughly worthwhile topic.

Amelia Carruthers

GEORGES GUYNEMER, KNIGHT OF THE AIR

TABLE OF CONTENTS

CANTO IV: THE ASCENSION

LIST OF ILLUSTRATIONS

INTRODUCTION

My dear M. Bordeaux:

I count the American people fortunate in reading any book of yours; I count them fortunate in reading any biography of that great hero of the air, Guynemer; and thrice over I count them fortunate to have such a book written by you on such a subject.

You, sir, have for many years been writing books peculiarly fitted to instill into your countrymen the qualities which during the last forty-eight months have made France the wonder of the world. You have written with such power and charm, with such mastery of manner and of matter, that the lessons you taught have been learned unconsciously by your readers — and this is the only way in which most readers will learn lessons at all. The value of your teachings would be as great for my countrymen as for yours. You have held up as an ideal for men and for women, that high courage which shirks no danger, when the danger is the inevitable accompaniment of duty. You have preached the essential virtues, the duty to be both brave and tender, the duty of courage for the man and courage for the woman. You have inculcated

9

stern horror of the baseness which finds expression
in refusal to perform those essential duties without
which not merely the usefulness, but the very
existence, of any nation will come to an end.

Under such conditions it is eminently appro-
priate that you should write the biography of that
soldier-son of France whose splendid daring has
made him stand as arch typical of the soul of the
French people through these terrible four years.
In this great war France has suffered more and has
achieved more than any other power. To her more
than to any other power, the final victory will be
due. Civilization has in the past, for immemorial
centuries, owed an incalculable debt to France;
but for no single feat or achievement of the past
does civilization owe as much to France as for what
her sons and daughters have done in the world war
now being waged by the free peoples against the
powers of the Pit.

Modern war makes terrible demands upon those
who fight. To an infinitely greater degree than ever
before the outcome depends upon long preparation
in advance, and upon the skillful and unified use of
the nation's entire social and industrial no less than
military power. The work of the general staff is infinitely more important than any work of the kind
in times past. The actual machinery of both is so
vast, delicate, and complicated that years are
needed to complete it. At all points we see the immense need of thorough organization and of making ready far in advance of the day of trial. But
this does not mean that there is any less need than

before of those qualities of endurance and hardihood, of daring and resolution, which in their sum make up the stern and enduring valor which ever has been and ever will be the mark of mighty victorious armies.

The air service in particular is one of such peril that membership in it is of itself a high distinction. Physical address, high training, entire fearlessness, iron nerve, and fertile resourcefulness are needed in a combination and to a degree hitherto unparalleled in war. The ordinary air fighter is an extraordinary man; and the extraordinary air fighter stands as one in a million among his fellows. Guynemer was one of these. More than this. He was the foremost among all the extraordinary fighters of all the nations who in this war have made the skies their battle field. We are fortunate indeed in having you write his biography.

Very faithfully yours,

(Signed) THEODORE ROOSEVELT.

M. HENRY BORDEAUX,
44 RUE DU RANELAGH,
PARIS, FRANCE.

PROLOGUE

"... GUYNEMER has not come back."

The news flew from one air escadrille to another, from the aviation camps to the troops, from the advance to the rear zones of the army; and a shock of pain passed from soul to soul in that vast army, and throughout all France, as if, among so many soldiers menaced with death, this one alone should have been immortal.

History gives us examples of such universal grief, but only at the death of great leaders whose authority and importance intensified the general mourning for their loss. Thus, Troy without Hector was defenseless. When Gaston de Foix, Duke de Nemours, surnamed the Thunderbolt of Italy, died at the age of twenty-three after the victory of Ravenna, the French transalpine conquests were endangered. The bullet which struck Turenne at Saltzbach also menaced the work of Louis XIV. But Guynemer had nothing but his airplane, a speck in the immense spaces filled by the war. This young captain, though without an equal in the sky, conducted no battle on land. Why, then, did he alone have the power, like a great military chief, of leaving universal sadness behind him? A little child of France has given us the reason.

13

Among the endless expressions of the nation's mourning, this letter was written by the schoolmistress of a village in Franche-Comté, Mademoiselle S——, of Bouclans, to the mother of the aviator:

Madame, you have already received the sorrowful and grateful sympathy of official France and of France as a nation; I am venturing to send you the naïve and sincere homage of young France as represented by our school children at Bouclans. Before receiving from our chiefs the suggestion, of which we learn to-day, we had already, on the 22d of October, consecrated a day to the memory of our hero Guynemer, your glorious son.

I send you enclosed an exercise by one of my pupils chosen at random, for all of them are animated by the same sentiments. You will see how the immortal glory of your son shines even in humble villages, and that the admiration and gratitude which the children, so far away in the country, feel for our greatest aviator, will be piously and faithfully preserved in his memory.

May this sincere testimony to the sentiments of childhood be of some comfort in your grief, to which I offer my most profound respect.

THE SCHOOL-MISTRESS OF BOUCLANS,

C. S.

And this is the exercise, written by Paul Bailly, aged eleven years and ten months:

Guynemer is the Roland of our epoch: like Roland he was very brave, and like Roland he died for France. But his exploits are not a legend like those of Roland, and in telling them just as they happened we find them more beautiful than any we could imagine. To do honor to him they are going to write his name in the Panthéon among the other great names. His airplane has been placed in the Invalides. In our school we consecrated a day to him. This morning as soon as we reached the school we put his photograph up on the wall; for our moral lesson we learned by heart his last mention in the despatches; for our writing lesson we wrote his name, and he was the subject for our theme; and finally, we had to draw an airplane. We did not begin to think of him only after he was dead; before he died, in our school, every time he brought down an airplane we were proud and happy. But when we heard that he was dead, we were as sad as if one of our own family had died.

Roland was the example for all the knights in history. Guynemer should be the example for Frenchmen now, and each one will try to imitate him and will remember him as we have remembered Roland. I, especially, I shall never forget him, for I shall remember that he died for France, like my dear Papa.

This little French boy's description of Guynemer is true and, limited as it is, sufficient: Guynemer is the modern Roland, with the same redoubtable youth and fiery soul. He is the last of the knights-errant, the first of the new knights of the air. His short life needs only accurate telling to appear like a legend. The void he left is so great because every household had adopted him. Each one shared in his victories, and all have written his name among their own dead.

Guynemer's glory, to have so ravished the minds of children, must have been both simple and per-

fect, and as his biographer I cannot dream of
equaling the young Paul Bailly. But I shall not
take his hero from him. Guynemer's life falls naturally into the legendary rhythm, and the simple and
exact truth resembles a fairy tale.

The writers of antiquity have mourned in touching accents the loss of young men cut down in the
flower of their youth. "The city," sighs Pericles,
"has lost its light, the year has lost its spring."
Theocritus and Ovid in turn lament the short life
of Adonis, whose blood was changed into flowers.
And in Virgil the father of the gods, whom Pallas
supplicates before facing Turnus, warns him not to
confound the beauty of life with its length:

Stat sua cuique dies; breve et irreparabile tempus
Omnibus est vitae; sed famam extendere factis,
Hoc virtutis opus. . ."

"The days of man are numbered, and his life-
time short and irrecoverable; but to increase his
renown by the quality of his acts, this is the work
of virtue. . ." [1]

Famam extendere factis: no fabulous personage of
antiquity made more haste than Guynemer to
multiply the exploits that increased his glory. But
the enumeration of these would not furnish a key
to his life, nor explain either that secret power he
possessed or the fascination he exerted. "It is not
always the most brilliant actions which best expose
the virtues or vices of men. Some trifle, some in-
significant word or jest, often displays the char-

[1] *Æneid*, Book 10, Garnier ed.

acter better than bloody combats, pitched battles, or the taking of cities. Also, as portrait painters try to reproduce the features and expression of their subjects, as the most obvious presentment of their characters, and without troubling about the other parts of the body, so we may be allowed to concentrate our study upon the distinctive signs of the soul. . . ." [1]

I, then, shall especially seek out these "distinctive signs of the soul."

Guynemer's family has confided to me his letters, his notebooks of flights, and many precious stories of his childhood, his youth, and his victories. I have seen him in camps, like the Cid Campeador, who made "the swarm of singing victories fly, with wings outspread, above his tents." I have had the good fortune to see him bring down an enemy airplane, which fell in flames on the bank of the river Vesle. I have met him in his father's house at Compiègne, which was his Bivar. Almost immediately after his disappearance I passed two night-watches — as if we sat beside his body — with his comrades, talking of nothing but him: troubled night-watches in which we had to change our shelter, for Dunkirk and the aviation field were bombarded by moonlight. In this way I was enabled to gather much scattered evidence, which will help, perhaps, to make clear his career. But I fear — and offer my excuses for this — to disappoint professional members of the aviation corps, who will find neither technical details nor the competence

[1] Plutarch, *Life of Alexander.*

of the specialist. One of his comrades of the air, —
and I hope it may be one of his rivals in glory, —
should give us an account of Guynemer in action.
The biography which I have attempted to write
seeks the soul for its object rather than the motor:
and the soul, too, has its wings.

France consented to love herself in Guynemer,
something which she is not always willing to do. It
happens sometimes that she turns away from her
own efforts and sacrifices to admire and celebrate
those of others, and that she displays her own
defects and wounds in a way which exaggerates
them. She sometimes appears to be divided against
herself; but this man, young as he was, had recon-
ciled her to herself. She smiled at his youth and
his prodigious deeds of valor. He made peace
within her; and she knew this, when she had lost
him, by the outbreak of her grief. As on the first
day of the war, France found herself once more
united; and this love sprang from her recognition
in Guynemer of her own impulses, her own
generous ardor, her own blood whose course has
not been retarded by many long centuries.

Since the outbreak of war there are few homes in
France which have not been in mourning. But
these fathers and mothers, these wives and children, when they read this book, will not say:
"What is Guynemer to us? Nobody speaks of *our*
dead." Their dead were, generally, infantry soldiers whom it was impossible for them to help,
whose life they only knew by hearsay, and whose
place of burial they sometimes do not know. So

many obscure soldiers have never been commemo-
rated, who gave, like Guynemer, their hearts and
their lives, who lived through the worst days of
misery, of mud and horror, and upon whom not the
least ray of glory has ever descended! The infantry
soldier is the pariah of the war, and has a right to
be sensitive. The heaviest weight of suffering
caused by war has fallen upon him. Nevertheless,
he had adopted Guynemer, and this was not the
least of the conqueror's conquests. The infantry-
man had not been jealous of Guynemer; he had felt
his fascination, and instinctively he divined a fra-
ternal Guynemer. When the French official dispatches reported the marvelous feats of the aviation
corps, the infantry soldier smiled scornfully in his
mole's-hole:

"Them again! Everlastingly them! And what
about us?"

But when Guynemer added another exploit to
his account, the trenches exulted, and counted over
again all his feats.

He himself, from his height, looked down in the
most friendly way upon these troglodytes who followed him with their eyes. One day when somebody
reproached him with running useless risks in aërial
acrobatic turns, he replied simply:

"After certain victories it is quite impossible not
to pirouette a bit, one is so happy!"

This is the spirit of youth. "They jest and play
with death as they played in school only yesterday
at recreation."[1] But Guynemer immediately added:

[1] Henri Lavedan (*L'Illustration* of October 6, 1917).

"It gives so much pleasure to the poilus watching us down there." [1]

The sky-juggler was working for his brother the infantryman. As the singing lark lifts the peasant's head, bent over his furrow, so the conquering airplane, with its overturnings, its "loopings," its close veerings, its spirals, its tail spins, its "zooms," its dives, all its tricks of flight, amuses for a while the sad laborers in the trenches.

May my readers, when they have finished this little book, composed according to the rules of the boy, Paul Bailly, lift their heads and seek in the sky whither he carried, so often and so high, the tricolor of France, an invisible and immortal Guynemer!

[1] Pierre l'Ermite (*La Croix* of October 7, 1917).

CANTO I

CHILDHOOD

I. THE GUYNEMERS

IN his book on Chivalry, the good Léon Gautier, beginning with the knight in his cradle and wishing to surround him immediately with a supernatural atmosphere, interprets in his own fashion the sleeping baby smiling at the angels. "According to a curious legend, the origin of which has not as yet been clearly discovered," he explains, "the child during its slumber hears 'music,' the incomparable music made by the movement of the stars in their spheres. Yes, that which the most illustrious scholars have only been able to suspect the existence of is distinctly heard by these ears scarcely opened as yet, and ravishes them. A charming fable, giving to innocence more power than to proud science." [1]

The biographer of Guynemer would like to be able to say that our new knight also heard in his cradle the music of the stars, since he was to be summoned to approach them. But it can be said, at least, that during his early years he saw the shadowy train of all the heroes of French history, from Charlemagne to Napoleon.

[1] *La Chevalerie*, by Léon Gautier. A. Walter ed. 1895.

Georges Marie Ludovic Jules Guynemer was born in Paris one Christmas Eve, December 24, 1894. He saw then, and always, the faces of three women, his mother and his two elder sisters, standing guard over his happiness. His father, an officer (Junior Class '80, Saint-Cyr), had resigned in 1890. An ardent scholar, he became a member of the Historical Society of Compiègne, and while examining the charters of the *Cartulaire de royallieu*, or writing a monograph on the *Seigneurie d'Offémont*, he verified family documents of the genealogy of his family. Above all, it was he in reality who educated his son.

Guynemer is a very old French name. In the *Chanson de Roland* one Guinemer, uncle of Ganelon, helped Roland to mount at his departure. A Guinemer appears in *Gaydon* (the knight of the jay), which describes the sorrowful return of Charlemagne to Aix-la-Chapelle after the drama of Roncevaux; and a Guillemer figures in *Fier-à-Bras*, in which Charlemagne and the twelve peers conquer Spain. This Guillemer l'Escot is made prisoner along with Oliver, Bérart de Montdidier, Auberi de Bourgoyne, and Geoffroy l'Angevin.

In the eleventh century the family of Guynemer left Flanders for Brittany. When the French Revolution began, there were still Guynemers in Brittany,[1] but the greatgrandfather of our hero,

---

[1] There are still Guynemers there. M. Etienne Dupont, Judge in the Civil Court of Saint-Malo, sent me an extract from an *aveu collectif* of the "Leftenancy of Tinténiac de Guinemer des Rabines." The Guynemers, in more recent

Bernard, was living in Paris in reduced circumstances, giving lessons in law. Under the Empire he was later to be appointed President of the Tribunal at Mayence, the chief town in the country of Mont Tonnerre. Falling into disfavor after 1815, he was only President of the Tribunal of Gannat.

Here, thanks to an unusual circumstance, oral tradition takes the place of writings, charters, and puzzling trifles. One of the four sons of Bernard Guynemer, Auguste, lived to be ninety-three, retaining all his faculties. Toward the end he resembled Voltaire, not only in face, but in his irony and skepticism. He had all sorts of memories of the Revolution, the Empire, and the Restoration, of which he told extraordinary anecdotes. His longevity was owing to his having been discharged from military service at the conscription. Two of his three brothers died before maturity: one, Alphonse, infantry officer, was killed at Vilna in 1812, and the other, Jules, naval officer, died in 1802 as the result of wounds received at Trafalgar. The last son, Achille, whom we shall presently refer to again, was to perpetuate the family name.

Auguste Guynemer remembered very vividly the day when he faced down Robespierre. He was at that time eight years old, and the mistress of his school had been arrested. He came to the school as usual and found there were no classes. Where

times, have left traces in the county of Saint-Malo, where Mgr. Guynemer de la Hélandière inaugurated, in September, 1869, the Tour Saint-Joseph, house of the Little Sisters of the Poor in Saint-Pern.

was his teacher? he asked. At the Revolutionary
Tribunal. Where was the Revolutionary Tribunal?
Jestingly they told him where to find it, and he
went straight to the place, entered, and asked back
the captive. The audience looked at the little boy
with amazement, while the judges joked and
laughed at him. But without being discomposed,
he explained the purpose of his visit. The incident
put Robespierre in good humor, and he told the
child that his teacher had not taught him anything.
Immediately, as a proof of the contrary, the
youngster began to recite his lessons. Robespierre
was so delighted that, in the midst of general
laughter, he lifted up the boy and kissed him. The
prisoner was restored to him, and the school reopened.

However, of the four sons of the President
of Mayence, the youngest only, Achille, was destined to preserve the family line. Born in 1792, a
volunteer soldier at the age of fifteen, his military
career was interrupted by the fall of the Empire. He
died in Paris, in the rue Rossini, in 1866. Edmond
About, who had known his son at Saverne, wrote
the following biographical notice:

A child of fifteen years enlisted as a Volunteer in
1806. Junot found him intelligent, made him his secretary, and took him to Spain. The young man won his
epaulettes under Colonel Hugo in 1811. He was made
prisoner on the capitulation of Guadalajara in 1812,
but escaped with two of his comrades whom he saved
at the peril of his own life. Love, or pity, led a young
Spanish girl to aid in this heroic episode, and for several

days the legend threatened to become a romance. But
the young soldier reappeared in 1813 at the passage of
the Bidassoa, where he was promoted lieutenant in the
4th Hussars, and was given the Cross by the Emperor,
who seldom awarded it. The return of the Bourbons
suddenly interrupted this career, so well begun. The
young cavalry officer then undertook the business of
maritime insurance, earning honorably a large fortune,
which he spent with truly military generosity, strewing
his road with good deeds. He continued working up to
the very threshold of death, for he resigned only a
month ago, and it was yesterday, Thursday, that we
laid him in his tomb at the age of seventy-five.

His name was Achille Guynemer. His family is
related to the Benoist d'Azy, the Dupré de Saint-Maur,
the Cochin, de Songis, du Trémoul and Vasselin
families, who have left memories of many exemplary
legal careers passed in Paris. His son, who wept yesterday as a child weeps before the tomb of such a father, is
the new Sub-Prefect of Saverne, the young and laborious
administrator who, from the beginning, won our gratitude and friendship.

The story of the escape from Spain contributes
another page to the family traditions. The young
Spanish girl had sent the prisoner a silken cord
concealed in a pie. A fourth companion in cap-
tivity was unfortunately too large to pass through
the vent-hole of the prison, and was shot by the
English. It was August 31, 1813, after the passage
of the Bidassoa, that Lieutenant Achille Guynemer
was decorated with the Cross of the Legion of
Honor. He was then twenty-one years of age. His
greatgrandson, who resembled the portraits of

Achille (especially a drawing done in 1807), at least in the proud carriage of the head, was to receive the Cross at an even earlier age.

There were other epic souvenirs which awakened Georges Guynemer's curiosity in childhood. He was shown the sword and snuffbox of General Count de Songis, brother of his paternal grandmother. This sword of honor had been presented to the general by the Convention when he was merely a captain of artillery, for having saved the cannon of the fortress at Valenciennes, — though it is quite true that Dumouriez, for the same deed, wished to have him hanged. The snuffbox was given him by the Emperor for having commanded the passage of the Rhine during the Ulm campaign.

Achille Guynemer had two sons. The elder, Amédée, a graduate of the École polytechnique, died at the age of thirty and left no children. The second, Auguste, was Sub-Prefect of Saverne under the Second Empire; and, resigning this office after the war of 1870, he became Vice-President of the society for the protection of Alsatians and Lorrainers, the President of which was the Count d'Haussonville. He had married a young Scottish lady, Miss Lyon, whose family included the Earls of Strathmore, among whose titles were those of Glamis and Cawdor mentioned by Shakespeare in "Macbeth."

As we have already seen, only one of the four sons of the President of Mayence — the hero of the Bidassoa — had left descendants. His son is M. Paul Guynemer, former officer and historian of the

Cartulaire de Royallieu and of the *Seigneurie d'Offémont*, whose only son was the aviator. The race whose history is lost far back in the *Chanson de Roland* and the Crusades, which settled in Flanders, and then in Brittany, but became, as soon as it left the provinces for the capital, nomadic, changing its base at will from the garrison of the officer to that of the official, seems to have narrowed and refined its stock and condensed all the power of its past, all its hopes for the future, in one last offshoot.

There are some plants, like the aloe, which bear but one flower, and sometimes only at the end of a hundred years. They prepare their sap, which has waited so long, and then from the heart of the plant issues a long straight stem, like a tree whose regular branches look like forged iron. At the top of this stem opens a marvelous flower, which is moist and seems to drop tears upon the leaves, inviting them to share its grief for the doom it awaits. When the flower is withered, the miracle is never renewed.

Guynemer is the flower of an old French family. Like so many other heroes, like so many peasants who, in this Great War, have been the wheat of the nation, his own acts have proved his nobility. But the fairy sent to preside at his birth laid in his cradle certain gilded pages of the finest history in the world: Roland, the Crusades, Brittany and Duguesclin, the Empire, and Alsace.

II. HOME AND COLLEGE

One of the generals best loved by the French troops, General de M——, a learned talker and charming moralist, who always seemed in his conversation to wander through the history of France, like a sorcerer in a forest, weaving and multiplying his spells, once recited to me the short prayer he had composed for grace to enable him to rear his children in the best way:

"Monseigneur Saint Louis, Messire Duguesclin, Messire Bayard, help me to make my sons brave and truthful."

So was Georges Guynemer reared, in the cult of truth, and taught that to deceive is to lower oneself. Even in his infancy he was already as proud as any personage. His early years were protected by the gentle and delicate care of his mother and his two sisters, who hung adoringly over him and were fascinated by his strange black eyes. What was to become of a child whose gaze was difficult to endure, and whose health was so fragile, for when only a few months old he had almost died of infantile enteritis. His parents had been obliged to carry him hastily to Switzerland, and then to Hyères, and to keep him in an atmosphere like that of a hothouse. Petted and spoiled, tended by women, like Achilles at Scyros among the daughters of Lycomedes, would he not bear all his life the stamp of too softening an education? Too pretty and too frail, with his curls and his dainty little frock, he had an *air de princesse*. His father felt that a mistake was being made, and that this excess of tenderness must be promptly ended. He took the child on his knees; a scene as trifling as it was decisive was about to be enacted:

"I almost feel like taking you with me, where I am going."

"Where are you going, father?"

"There, where I am going, there are only men."

"I want to go with you."

The father seemed to hesitate, and then to decide:

"After all, too early is better than too late. Put on your hat. I shall take you." He took him to the hairdresser.

"I am going to have my hair cut. How do you feel about it?"

"I want to do like men."

The child was set upon a stool where, in the white combing-cloth, with his curly hair, he resembled an angel done by an Italian Primitive. For an instant the father thought himself a barbarian, and the barber hesitated, scissors in air, as before a crime. They exchanged glances; then the father stiffened and gave the order. The beautiful curls fell.

But now it became necessary to return home; and when his mother saw him, she wept.

"I am a man," the child announced, peremptorily.

He was indeed to be a man, but he was to remain for a long time also a mischievous boy — nearly, in fact, until the end.

When he was six or seven years old he began to
study with the teacher of his sisters, which was
convenient and agreeable, but meant the addition
of another petticoat. The fineness of his feelings,
his fear of having wounded any comrade, which
were later to inspire him in so many touching
actions, were the result of this feminine education.
His walks with his father, who already gave him
much attention, brought about useful reactions.
Compiègne is rich in the history of the past: kings
were crowned there, and kings died there. The
Abbey of Saint Cornille sheltered, perhaps, the holy
winding-sheet of Christ. Treaties were signed at
Compiègne, and there magnificent fêtes were given
by Louis XIV, Louis XV, Napoleon I, and Napoleon III. And even in 1901 the child met Czar
Nicholas and Czarina Alexandra, who were staying
there. So, the palace and the forest spoke to him of
a past which his father could explain. And on the
Place de l'Hôtel de Ville he was much interested in
the bronze statue of the young girl, bearing a
banner.

"Who is it?"

"Jeanne d'Arc."

Georges Guynemer's parents renounced the
woman teacher, and in order to keep him near
them, entered him as a day scholar at the lyceum
of Compiègne. Here the child worked very little.
M. Paul Guynemer, having been educated at
Stanislas College, in Paris, wished his son also to go
there. Georges was then twelve years old.

"In a photograph of the pupils of the Fifth

(green) Class," wrote a journalist in the *Journal des
Débats*, who had had the curiosity to investigate
Georges' college days, "may be seen a restless-
looking little boy, thinner and paler than the others,
whose round black eyes seem to shine with a som-
ber brilliance. These eyes, which, eight or ten years
later, were to hunt and pursue so many enemy
airplanes, are passionately self-willed. The same
temperament is evident in a snapshot of this same
period, in which Georges is seen playing at war.
The college registers of this year tell us that he had
a clear, active, well-balanced mind, but that he was
thoughtless, mischief-making, disorderly, careless;
that he did not work, and was undisciplined, though
without any malice; that he was very proud, and
'ambitious to attain first rank': a valuable guide
in understanding the character of one who became
'the ace of aces.' In fact, at the end of the year
young Guynemer received the first prize for Latin
translation, the first prize for arithmetic, and four
honorable mentions."

The author of the *Débats* article, who is a scholar,
recalls Michelet's *mòt:* "The Frenchman is that
naughty child characterized by the good mother
of Duguesclin as 'the one who is always fighting the
others. . . .'" But the best portrait of Guynemer as
a child I find in the unpublished notes of Abbé
Chesnais, who was division prefect at Stanislas
College during the four years which Guynemer
passed there. The Abbé Chesnais had divined this
impassioned nature, and watched it with troubled
sympathy.

"His eyes vividly expressed the headstrong, fighting nature of the boy," he says of his pupil. "He did not care for quiet games, but was devoted to those requiring skill, agility, and force. He had a decided preference for a game highly popular among the younger classes — *la petite guerre*. The class was divided into two armies, each commanded by a general chosen by the pupils themselves, and having officers of all ranks under his orders. Each soldier wore on his left arm a movable brassard. The object of the battle was the capture of the flag, which was set up on a wall, a tree, a column, or any place dominating the courtyard. The soldier from whom his brassard was taken was considered dead.

"Guynemer, who was somewhat weak and sickly, always remained a private soldier. His comrades, appreciating the value of having a general with sufficient muscular strength to maintain his authority, never dreamed of placing him at their head. The muscle, which he lacked, was a necessity. But when a choice of soldiers had to be made, he was always counted among the best, and his name called among the first. Although he had not much strength, he had agility, cleverness, a quick eye, caution, and a talent for strategy. He played his game himself, not liking to receive any suggestions from his chiefs, intending to follow his own ideas. The battle once begun, he invariably attacked the strongest enemy and pursued those comrades who occupied the highest rank. With the marvelous suppleness of a cat, he climbed trees, flung himself to the ground, crept along barriers, slipped between the legs of his adversaries, and bounded triumphantly off with a number of brassards. It was a great joy to him to bring the trophies of his struggles to his general. With radiant face, and with his two hands resting on his legs, he looked mockingly at his adversaries who had been surprised by his cleverness. His superiority over his comrades was especially apparent in the battles they fought in the woods of Bellevue.[1] There the field was larger, and there was a greater variety of chances for surprising the enemy. He hid himself under the dead leaves, lay close to the branches of trees, and crept along brooks and ravines. It was often he who was selected to find a place of vantage for the flag. But he was never willing to act as its guardian, for he feared nothing so much as inactivity, preferring to chase his comrades through the woods. The short journey to the Bellevue woods was passed in the elaboration of various plans, and arguing about those of his friends; he always wanted to have the last word. The return journey was enlivened by biting criticism, which often ended in a quarrel."[2]

This is an astonishing portrait, in which nearly all the characteristics of the future Guynemer, Guynemer the fighter, are apparent. He does not care to command, he likes too well to give battle, and is already the knight of single combats. His

[1] The country house of Stanislas College is at Bellevue. [Translator's note.]

[2] Unpublished notes by Abbé Chesnais.

method is personal, and he means to follow his own ideas. He attacks the strongest; neither size nor number stops him. His suppleness and skill are unequaled. He lacks the muscle for a good gymnast, and at the parallel bars, or the fixed bar, he is the despair of his instructors. How will he supply this deficiency? Simply by the power of his will. All physical games do not require physical strength, and he became an excellent shot and fencer. Furious at his own weakness, he outdid the strong, and, like Diomede and Ajax, brought back his trophies laughing. A college courtyard was not sufficient for him: he needed the Bellevue woods, while he waited to have all space, all the sky, at his disposal. So the warlike infancy of a Guynemer is like that of a Roland, a Duguesclin, a Bayard, — all are ardent hearts with indomitable energy, upright souls developing early, whose passion it was only necessary to control.

The youth of Guynemer was like his childhood. As a student of higher mathematics his combative tendencies were not at all changed. "At recreation he was very fond of roller-skating, which in his case gave rise to many disputes and much pugilism. Having no respect for boys who would not play, he would skate into the midst of their group, pushing them about, seizing their arms and forcing them to waltz round and round with him like weathercocks. Then he would be off at his highest speed, pursued by his victims. Blows were exchanged, which did not prevent him from repeating the same thing a few seconds later. At the end of recreation, with his hair disordered, his clothes covered with dust, his face and hands muddy, Guynemer was exhausted. But the strongest of his comrades could not frighten him; on the contrary, he attacked these by preference. The masters were often obliged to intervene and separate the combatants. Guynemer would then straighten up like a cock, his eyes sparkling and obtruding, and, unable to do more, would crush his adversary with piquant and sometimes cutting words uttered in a dry, railing voice." [1]

Talking, however, was not his forte, and his nervousness made him sputter. His speech was vibrant, trenchant, like hammerstrokes, and he said things to which there was no answer. He had a horror of discussion: he was already all action.

This violence and frenzied action would have driven him to the most unreasonable and dangerous audacity if they had not been counterbalanced by his sense of honor. "He was one of those," wrote a comrade of Guynemer's, M. Jean Constantin, now lieutenant of artillery, "for whom honor is sacred, and must not be disregarded under any pretext; and in his life, in his relations with his comrades, his candor and loyalty were only equaled by his goodness. Often, in the midst of our games, some dispute arose. Where are the friends who have never had a dispute? Sometimes we were both so obstinate that we fought, but after that he was willing to renounce the privilege of the last word. He never could have endured bringing trouble

[1] Unpublished notes by Abbé Chesnais.

upon his fellow-students. He never hesitated to admit a fault; and, what is much better, once when one of his comrades, who was a good student, had inadvertently made a foolish mistake which might have lowered his marks, I saw Georges accuse himself and take the punishment in his place. His comrade never knew anything about it, for Georges did that sort of thing almost clandestinely, and with the simplicity and modesty which were always the great charm of his character."

This sense of honor he had drawn in with his mother's milk; and his father had developed it in him. Everything about him indicated pride: the upright carriage of his head, the glance of his black eyes which seemed to pierce the objects he looked at. He loved the Stanislas uniform which his father had worn before him, and which had been worn by Gouraud and Baratier, whose fame was then increasing, and Rostand, then in all the new glory of *Cyrano* and *L'Aiglon*. He had an exact appreciation of his own dignity. Though he listened attentively in class, he would never ask for information or advice from his classmates. He hated to be trifled with, and made it understood that he intended to be respected. Never in all his life did he have a low thought. If he ever varied from the nobleness which was natural to him, silence was sometimes sufficient to bring him to himself.

With a mobile face, full of contrasts, he was sometimes the roguish boy who made the whole' class shake with laughter, and involved it in a whirlwind of games and tricks, and at others the

serious, thoughtful pupil, who was considered to
be self-absorbed, distant, and not inclined to reveal
himself to anybody. The fierce soldier of the *petite
guerre* was also a formidable adversary at checkers.
Here, however, he became patient, only moving
his pieces after long reflection. None of the students could beat him, and no one could take him
by surprise. If he was beaten by a professor, he
never rested until he had had his revenge. His
power of will was far beyond his years, but it
needed to be relaxed. To study and win to the
head of his class was nothing for his lively intelligence, but his health was always delicate. He would
appear wrapped in cloaks, comforters, waterproof
coats, and then vanish into the infirmary. This
boy who did not fear blows, bruises, or falls, was
compelled to avoid draughts and to diet. Nobody
ever heard him complain, nor was any one ever to
do so. Often he had to give up work for whole
months at a time; and in his baccalaureate year he
was stopped by a return of the infantile enteritis.
"Three months of rest," the doctor ordered at
Christmas. "You will do your rhetoric over again
next year," said his father, who came to take
him home. "Not at all," said the boy; "the boys
shall not get ahead of me" — a childish boast
which passed unnoticed. At the end of three months
of rest and pleasant walks around Compiègne, the
child remarked: "The three months are up, and I
mean to present myself in July." "You haven't
time; it is impossible." He insisted. So they discovered, at Compiègne, the Pierre d'Ailly school,

in a building which since then has been ruined by a shell. It was his idea to attend these classes as a day scholar, just for the pleasure of it. He promised to continue to take care of himself at home. And in the month of July, at the age of fifteen, he took his bachelor degree, with mention.

But the bow cannot long remain bent, and hence certain diversions of his, ending sometimes in storms, but not caused by any ill-will on his part, for it was repugnant to him to give others pain. The following autumn he returned to Stanislas College, and resumed his school exploits.

"Vexed to find that a place had been reserved for him near the professor, under the certainly justified pretext that he was too much inclined to talk," again writes Abbé Chesnais, "he was resolved to talk all the same, whenever he pleased. With the aid of pins, pens, wires and boxes, he soon set up a telephone which put him into communication with the boy whose desk was farthest away. He possessed tools necessary for any of his tricks, and his desk was a veritable bazaar: copybooks, books, pen-holders and paper were mixed pell-mell with the most unlikely objects, such as fragments of fencing foils, drugs, chemical products, oil, grease, bolts, skate wheels, and tablets of chocolate. In one corner, carefully concealed, were some glass tubes which awaited a favorable moment for projecting against the ceiling a ball of chewed paper. Attached to this ball, a paper personage cut out of a copybook cover danced feverishly in space. When this grotesque figurine became quiet, another paper ball, shot with great skill, renewed the dancing to the great satisfaction of the young marksman. Airplanes made of paper were also hidden in this desk, awaiting the propitious hour for launching them; and the professor's desk sometimes served as their landing place. . . . Everything, indeed, was to be found there, but in such disorder that the owner himself could never find them. Who has not seen him hunting for a missing exercise in a copybook full of scraps of paper? It is time to go to class; with his head hidden in his desk, he turns over all its contents in great haste, upsetting a badly closed ink-bottle over his books and copybooks. The master calls him to order, and he rushes out well behind all the rest of the boys.

"He was not one of those ill-intentioned boys whose sole idea is to disturb the class and hinder the work of his comrades. Nor was he a ringleader. He acted entirely on his own account, and for his own satisfaction. His practical jokes never lasted long, and did not interrupt the work of others. His upright, frank and honest nature always led him to acknowledge his own acts when the master attributed them by mistake to the wrong boys. He never allowed any comrade to take his punishment for him, but he knew very well how to extricate himself from the greatest difficulties. His candor often won him some indulgence. If he happened to be punished by a timorous master, he assumed a terrible facial expression and tried to frighten him. But when, on the contrary, he found himself in the presence of a man of energy, he pleaded extenuating circumstances, and persevered until he obtained the least possible punishment. He never resented the infliction of just punishment, but suffered very much when punished in public. On the day when the class marks were read aloud, if he suspected that his own were to be bad, he took refuge in the infirmary to avoid the shame of public exposure. Honor, for him, was not a vain word.

"He was very sensitive to reproaches. He was an admirer of courage, audacity, anything generous. Who at Stanislas does not remember his proud and haughty attitude when a master vexed him in presence of his classmates, or interfered to end a quarrel in which his own self-respect was at stake? All his nerves were stretched; his body stiffened, and he stood as straight as a steel rod, his arms pressed against his legs, his fists tightly closed, his head held high and rigid, and his face as yellow as ivory, with its smooth forehead, and his compressed lips cutting two deep lines around his mouth; his eyes, fixed like two black balls, seemed to start from the sockets, shooting fire. He looked as if he were about to destroy his adversary with lightning, but in reality he retained the most imperturbable sang-froid. He stood like a marble statue, but it was easy to divine the storm raging within...." [1]

His tendency, after taking his bachelor's degree, was towards science; he was ambitious to enter the École polytechnique, and joined the special mathematics class. Even when very young he had shown particular aptitude for mechanics, and a gift for

---

[1] Unpublished notes by Abbé Chesnais.

invention which we have seen exercised in his practical jokes as a student. When he was only four or five years old he constructed a bed out of paper, which he raised by means of cords and pulleys.

"He passed whole hours," says his Stanislas classmate, Lieutenant Constantin, "in trying to solve a mathematical problem, or studying some question which had interested him, without knowing what went on around him; but as soon as he had solved his problem, or learned something new, he was satisfied and returned to the present. He was particularly interested in everything connected with the sciences. His greatest pleasure was to make experiments in physics or chemistry: he tried everything which his imagination suggested. Once he happened to produce a detonating mixture which made a formidable explosion, but nothing was broken except a few windows."

His choice of reading revealed the same tendency. He was not fond of reading, and only liked books of adventure which were food for his warlike sentiments and his ideas of honor and honesty. He preferred the works of Major Driant, and re-read them even during his mathematical year. Returning from a walk one Thursday evening, he knocked on the prefect's door to ask for a book. He wanted *La Guerre fatale*, *La Guerre de Demain*, *L'Aviateur du Pacifique*, etc. "But you have already read them." "That does not matter." Did he really re-read them? His dreams were always the same, and his eyes looked into the future.

Somebody, however, was to exert over this impressionable, mobile, almost too ardent nature, an influence which was to determine its direction. His father had advised him to choose his friends with care, and not yield himself to the first comer. He was not only incapable of doing that, but equally incapable of yielding himself to anybody. Do we really choose our friends in early life? We only know our friends by finding them in our lives when we need them. They are there, but we have not sought them. A similarity of taste, of sensibility, of ambitions draw us to them, and they have been our friends a long time already before we perceive that they are not merely comrades. Thus Jean Krebs became the constant companion of Georges Guynemer. The father of Jean Krebs is that Colonel Krebs whose name is connected with the first progress made in aërostation and aviation. He was then director of the Panhard factories, and his two sons were students at Stanislas. Jean, the elder, was Guynemer's classmate. He was a silent, self-centered, thoughtful student, calm in speech and facial expression, never speaking one word louder than another, and the farthest possible removed from anything noisy or agitated. Georges broke in upon his solitude and attached himself to him, while Krebs endured, smiled, and accepted, and they became allies. It was Krebs, for the time, who was the authority, the one who had prestige and wore the halo. Why, he knew what an automobile was, and one Sunday he took his friend Georges to Ivry and taught him how to drive.

He taught him every technical thing he knew. Georges launched with all his energy into this new career, and soon became acquainted with every motor in existence. During the school promenades, if the column of pupils walked up or down the Champs Elysées, he told them the names of passing automobiles: "That's a Lorraine. There is a Panhard. This one has so many horsepower," etc. Woe to any who ventured to contradict him. He looked the insolent one up and down, and crushed him with a word.

He was overjoyed when the college organized Thursday afternoon visits to factories. He chose his companions in advance, sometimes compelling them to give up a game of tennis. Krebs was one of them. For Georges the visits to the Puteaux and Dion-Bouton factories were a feast of which he was often to speak later. He went, not as a sightseer, but as a connoisseur. He could not bring himself to remain with the engineer who showed the party through the works. He required more liberty, more time to investigate everything for himself, to see and touch everything. The smallest detail interested him; he questioned the workmen, asking them the use of some screw, and a thousand other things. The visit was too soon over for him; and when his comrades had already left, and the division prefect was calling the roll to make sure of all his boys, Guynemer as usual was missing, and was discovered standing in ecstasy before a machine which some workmen were engaged in setting up.

"The opening weeks of the automobile and aviation exhibition were a period of comparative tranquillity for his masters, as Guynemer was no longer the same restless, nervous, mischievous boy, being too anxious to retain his privileges for the promenades. He was always one of those who haunted the prefect when the hour for departure drew near. He was impatient to know where they were to go: 'Where are we going?... Shall you take us to the Grand Palais? (The Automobile and Aviation Exhibition)... Wouldn't you be a brick! ...' When they arrived, he was not one of those many curious people who circulate aimlessly around the stands with their hands in their pockets, without reaping anything but fatigue, like a cyclist on a circular track. His plans were all made in advance, and he knew where the stand was which he meant to visit. He went directly there, where his ardor and his free and easy behavior drew upon him the admonitions of the proprietor. But nothing stopped him, and he continued to touch everything, furnishing explanations to his companions. When he returned to the college his pockets bulged with prospectuses, catalogues, and selected brochures, which he carefully added to the heterogeneous contents of his desk." [1]

Jean Krebs crystallized Georges Guynemer's vocation. He developed and specialized his taste for mechanics, separating it from vague abstractions and guiding it towards material realities and the wider experiences these procure. He deserves

[1] Unpublished notes by Abbé Chesnais.

to be mentioned in any biography of Guynemer, and before passing on, it is proper that his premature loss should be cited and deplored. Highly esteemed as an aviator during the war, he made the best use of his substantial and reliable faculties in the work of observation. Airplane chasing did not attract him, but he knew how to use his eyes. He was killed in a landing accident at a time almost coincident with the disappearance of Guynemer. One of his escadrille mates described him thus: "With remarkable intelligence, and a perfectly even disposition, his chiefs valued him for his sang-froid, his quick eye, his exact knowledge of the services he was able to perform. Every time a mission was intrusted to him, everybody was sure that he would accomplish it, no matter what conditions he had to meet. He often had to face enemy airplanes better armed than his own, and in the course of a flight had been wounded in the thigh by an exploding shell. Nevertheless he had continued to fly, only returning considerably later when his task was done. His death has left a great void in this escadrille. Men like him are difficult to replace. . . ."

Thus the immoderate Guynemer had for his first friend a comrade who knew exactly his own limits. Guynemer could save Jean Krebs from his excess of literal honesty by showing him the enchantment of his own ecstasies, but Jean Krebs furnished the motor for Guynemer's ambitious young wings. Without the technical lessons of Jean Krebs, could Guynemer later have got into the

aviation field at Pau, and won so easily his diploma
as pilot? Would he have applied himself so closely
to the study of his tools and the perfecting of his
machine?

The war was to make them both aviators, and
both of them fell from the sky, one in the fullness
of glory, the other almost obscure. When they
talked together on school outings, or as they
walked along beside the walls of Stanislas, had
they ever foreseen this destiny? Certainly not Jean
Krebs, with his positive spirit; he only saw ahead
the École polytechnique, and thought of nothing
but preparation for that. But Guynemer? In his
very precious notes, Abbé Chesnais shows us
the boy constructing a little airplane of cloth, the
motor of which was a bundle of elastics. "At the
next recreation hour, he went up to the dormitory,
opened a window, launched his machine, and pre-
sided over its evolutions above the heads of his
comrades." But these were only the games of an
ingenious collegian. The worthy priest, who was
division prefect, and watched the boy with a profound knowledge of psychology, never received
any confidence from him regarding his vocation.

Aviation, whose first timid essays began in 1906,
progressed rapidly. After Santos Dumont, who on
November 22, 1906, covered 220 meters while
volplaning, a group of inventors — Blériot, Dela-
grange, Farman, Wright — perfected light motors.
In 1909 Blériot crossed the Channel, Paulhan won
the height record at 1380 meters, and Farman the
distance record over a course of 232 kilometers.

A visionary, Viscomte Melchior de Vogué, had already foreseen the prodigious development of air-travel. All the young people of the time longed to fly. Guynemer, studying the new invention with his customary energy, could hardly do otherwise than share the general infatuation. His comrades, like himself, dreamed of parts of airplanes and their construction. But the idea of Lieutenant Constantin is different: "When an airplane flew over the quarter, Guynemer followed it with his eyes, and continued to gaze at the sky for some time after its disappearance. His desk contained a whole collection of volumes and photographs concerning aviation. He had resolved to go up some day in an airplane, and as he was excessively self-willed he tried to bring this about by every means in his power. 'Don't you know anybody who could take me up some Sunday?' Of whom has he not asked this question? But at college it was not at all easy, and it was during vacation that he succeeded in carrying out his project. If I am not mistaken, his first ascension was at the aërodrome of Compiègne. At that time the comfortable cockpits of the modern airplanes were unknown, and the passenger was obliged to place himself as best he could behind the pilot and cling to him by putting his arms around him in order not to fall, so that it was a relief to come down again! ..."

The noticeable sentence in these notes is the first one: *When an airplane flew over the quarter, he followed it with his eyes, and continued to gaze at the sky for some time after its disappearance.* If

Jean Krebs had survived, he could perhaps enlighten us still further; but, even to this reasonable friend, could Guynemer have revealed what was still confused to himself? Jean Constantin only saw him once in a reverie; and Guynemer must have kept silent about his resolutions.

Soon afterwards, as Guynemer was obliged once more to renounce his studies — and this was the year in which he was preparing for the Polytechnique — his father left him with his grandmother in Paris, to rest. During this time he went to lectures on the social sciences, finally completing his education, which was strictly French, not one day having been passed with any foreign teacher. After this he traveled with his mother and sisters, leading the life of the well-to-do young man who has plenty of time in which to plan his future. Was he thinking of his future at all? The question occurred to his father who, worried at the thought of his son's idleness, recalled him and interrogated him as to his ideas of a future career, fully expecting to receive one of those undecided answers so often given by young men under similar circumstances. But Georges replied, as if it were the most natural thing in the world, and no other could ever have been considered:

"Aviator."

This reply was surprising. What could have led him to a determination apparently so sudden?

"That is not a career," he was told. "Aviation is still only a sport. You travel in the air as a motorist rides on the highways. And after passing a few years devoted to pleasure, you hire yourself to some constructor. No, a thousand times no!"

Then he said to his father what he had never said to anybody, and what his comrade Constantin had merely suspected:

"That is my sole passion. One morning in the courtyard at Stanislas I saw an airplane flying. I don't know what happened to me: I felt an emotion so profound that it was almost religious. You must believe me when I ask your permission to be an aviator."

"You don't know what an airplane is. You never saw one except from below."

"You are mistaken; I went up in one at Corbeaulieu."

Corbeaulieu was an aërodome near Compiègne; and these words were spoken a very few months before the war.

Many years before Georges Guynemer was a student at Stanislas, a professor, who was also destined to become famous, taught rhetoric there. His name was Frédéric Ozanam. He too had been a precocious child, prematurely sure of his vocation for literature. When only fifteen he had composed in Latin verse an epitaph in honor of Gaston de Foix, dead at Ravenna. This epitaph, if two words are changed — *Hispanae* into *hostilis*, and *Gaston* into *Georges* — describes perfectly the short and admirable career of Guynemer. Even the palms are included:

Fortunate heros! moriendo in saecula vives.
Eia, agite, o socii, manibus profundite flores,
Lilia per tumulum, violamque rosamque recentem
Spargite; victricis armis superaddite lauros,
Et tumulo tales mucrone inscribite voces:
Hic jacet hostilis gentis timor et decus omne
      Gallorum, Georgius, conditus ante diem:
Credidit hunc Lachesis juvenem dum cerneret annos,
      Sed palmas numerans credidit esse senem.[1]

It is a paraphrase of the reply of the gods to
the young Pallas, in Virgil.

This young Frédéric Ozanam died in the full
vigor of manhood before having attained his
fortieth year, of a malady which had already fore-
told his death. At that time he seemed to have
achieved perfect happiness; it was the supreme
moment when everything succeeds, when the difficult years are almost forgotten, and the road
mounts easily upward. He had in his wife a perfect
companion, and his daughter was a lovable young
girl. His reputation was growing; he was soon to
be received by the Academy, and fortune and fame
were already achieved. And then death called
him.   Truly the hour was badly chosen — but

[1] Fortunate hero! thou diest, but thou shalt live forever!
Come, my companions! strew flowers
And lilies over the tomb! violets and young roses
Scatter; heap up laurels upon his arms,
And on the stone write with the point of your sword:
"Here lieth one who was the terror of the enemy, and the glory
Of the French, George, taken before his time.
Lachesis from his face thought him a boy,
But counting his victories she thought him full of years.

when is it chosen at the will of mortals? Ozanam
tried to win pity from death. In his private journal
he notes death's approach, concerning which he
was never deceived; and he asks Heaven for a
respite. To propitiate it, he offers a part of his life,
the most brilliant part; he is willing to renounce
honors, fame, and fortune, and will consent to live
humbly and be forgotten, like the poor for whom
he founded the *Conférences de Saint-Vincent de
Paul*, and whom he so often visited in their
wretched lodgings; but let him at least dwell a
little longer in his home, that he may see his
daughter grow up, and pass a few years more with
the companion of his choice. Finally, he is impassioned by his Faith, he no longer reasons with
Heaven, but says: "Take all according to Thy
wish, take all, take myself. Thy will be done. . . ."

Rarely has the drama of acceptance of the Divine
Will been more freely developed. Now, in the drama
which was to impassion Guynemer even to complete sacrifice, it is not the vocation of aviator that
we should remark, but the absolute will to serve.
Abbé Chesnais, who does not attach primary importance to the vocation, has understood this well.
At the end of his notes he reminds us that Guynemer was a believer who accomplished his religious
exercises regularly, without ostentation and without weakness. "How many times he has stopped
me at night," he writes, "as I passed near his bed!
He wanted a quiet conscience, without reproach.
His usual frivolity left him at the door of the
chapel. He believed in the presence of God in this

holy place and respected it. . . . His Christian sentiments were to be a sustaining power in his aërial
battles, and he would fight with the more ardor
if his conscience were at peace with his God. . . ."

These words of Abbé Chesnais explain the true
vocation of Guynemer: "The chances of war
brought out marvelously the qualities contained in
such a frail body. In the beginning did he think
of becoming a pilot? Perhaps. But what he wanted
above everything was to fulfil his duty as a
Frenchman. He wanted to be a soldier; he was
ashamed of himself, he said, in the first days of
September, 1914: 'If I have to sleep in the bottom
of an automobile truck, I want to go to the front.
I will go.'"

He was to go; but neither love of aviation nor
love of fame had anything to do with his departure,
as they were to have nothing to do with his final
fate.

III. THE DEPARTURE

In the month of July, 1914, Georges Guynemer
was with his family at the Villa Delphine, Biarritz,
in the northern part of the Anglet beach. This
beach is blond with sunshine, but is refreshed by
the ocean breezes. One can be deliciously idle there.
This beach is besides an excellent landing-place for
airplanes, because of the welcome of its soft sand.
Georges Guynemer never left the Anglet beach,
and every time an airplane descended he was there
to receive it. He was the aviation sentry. But at
this period airplanes were rare. Guynemer had his

own thoughts, and tenacity was one of his dominant traits; he was already one of those who never renounce. The bathers who passed this everlasting idler never suspected that he was obstinately developing one single plan, and hanging his whole future upon it.

Meanwhile the horizon of Europe darkened. Ever since the assassination of the Archduke Ferdinand of Austria, at Sarajevo, electricity had accumulated in the air, and the storm was ready to burst. To this young man, the Archduke and the European horizon were things of nothing. The sea-air was healthful, and he searched the heavens for invisible airplanes. The conversations in progress all around him were full of anxiety; he had no time to listen to them. The eyes of the women began to be full of pain; he did not notice the eyes of women. On the second of August the order for mobilization was posted. It was war!

Then Guynemer rid himself of his dream, as if it were something unreal, and broke off brusquely all his plans for the future. He was entirely possessed by another idea, which made his eyes snap fire, and wrinkled his forehead. He rushed to his father and without taking breath announced:

"I am going to enlist."

"You are lucky."

"Well, then, you authorize me. . . ."

"I envy you."

He had feared to be met with some parental objection on account of the uncertain health which had so often thwarted him, and had postponed his preparation for the École Polytechnique. Now he felt reassured. Next day he was at Bayonne, getting through all the necessary formalities. He was medically examined — and postponed. The doctors found him too tall, too thin — no physiological defect, but a child's body in need of being developed and strengthened. In vain he supplicated them; they were pitiless. He returned home grieved, humiliated, and furious. The Villa Delphine was to know some very uncomfortable days. His family understood his determination and began to have fears for him. And he returned to the charge, and attacked his father with insistence, as if his father were all-powerful and could, if he would, compel them to accept his son's services for *la Patrie*.

"If you would help me, I should not be put off."

"But how?"

"A former officer has connections in the army. You could speak for me."

"Very well, I will."

M. Guynemer, in his turn, went to Bayonne. From that date, indeed from the first day of war, he had promised himself never to set obstacles in the way of his son's military service, but to favor it upon all occasions. He kept his word, as we shall see later, at whatever cost to himself. The recruiting major listened to his request. It was the hour of quick enthusiasms, and he had already sustained many assaults and resisted many importunities.

"Monsieur," he now said, "you may well believe that I accept all who can serve. I speak to you as a former officer: does your conscience assure you that your son is fit to carry a knapsack and be a foot-soldier?"

"I could not say that he is."

"Would he make a cavalryman?"

"He can't ride on account of his former enteritis."

"Then you see how it is; it's proper to postpone him. Build him up, and later on he'll be taken. The war is not finished."

As Georges had been present at this interview, he now saw himself refused a second time. He returned with his father to Biarritz, pale, silent, unhappy, and altogether in such a state of anger and bitterness that his face was altered. Nothing consoled him, nothing amused him. On those magnificent August days the sea was a waste of sunshine, and the beach was an invitation to enjoy the soft summer hours; but he did not go to the beach, and he scorned the sea. His anxious parents wondered if, for the sake of his health, it would not be easier to see him depart. As for them, it was their fate to suffer in every way.

Ever since the mobilization, Georges Guynemer had had only one thought: to serve — to serve, no matter where, no matter how, no matter in what branch of the service, but to leave, to go to the front, and not stay there at Biarritz like those foreigners who had not left, or like those useless old men and children who were now all that remained of the male population.

Many trains had carried off the first recruits,

trains decorated with flowers and filled with songs. The sons of France had come running from her farthest provinces, and a unanimous impulse precipitated them upon the assaulted frontier. But this impulse was perfectly controlled. The songs the men sang were serious and almost sacred. The nation was living through one of her greatest hours, and knew it. With one motion she regained her national unity, and renewed once more her youth.

Meanwhile the news that sifted in, little by little, caused intense anguish — anguish, not doubt. The government had left Paris to establish itself at Bordeaux. The capital was menaced. The enemy had entered Compiègne. Compiègne was no longer ours. The Joan of Arc on the *place* of the Hôtel de Ville had *pickelhauben* on her men-at-arms. And then the victory of the Marne lifted the weight that oppressed every heart. At the Villa Delphine news came that Compiègne was saved. Meanwhile trains left carrying troops to reinforce the combatants. And Georges Guynemer had to live through all these departures, suffering and rebelling until he had a horror of himself. His comrades and friends were gone, or had asked permission to go. His two first cousins, his mother's nephews, Guy and René de Saint Quentin, had gone; one, a sergeant, was killed at the Battle of the Marne, the other, councilor to the Embassy at Constantinople, returning in haste when war was declared, had taken his place as lieutenant of reserves, and had been twice wounded at the Marne, by a ball in the shoulder and a shrapnel bullet in the thigh. Was it possible for him to stay there alone when the whole of France had risen?

In the *Chanson d'Aspremont,* which is one of our most captivating *chansons de geste,* Charlemagne is leaving for Italy with his army, and passes by Laon. In the donjon five children, one of whom is his nephew Roland, are imprisoned under the care of Turpin. The Emperor, who knows them well, has had them locked up for fear they would join his troops. But when they hear the ivory horns sounding and the horses neighing, they are determined to escape. They try to cajole the porter, but he is adamant and incorruptible. This faithful servitor is immediately well beaten. They take away his keys, pass over his body, and are soon out of the prison. But their adventures are only beginning. To procure themselves horses they attack and unhorse five Bretons, and to get arms they repeat the same process. They are so successful that they manage to join the Emperor's army before it has crossed the Alps. Will our new Roland allow himself to be outdistanced by these terrible children of former ages? It is not the army with its ivory horns that he has heard departing, but the whole marching nation, fighting to live and endure, and to enable honor and justice and right to live and endure with her.

So we find Guynemer once more on the Anglet beach, sad and discomfited. An airplane capsizes on the sand. What does he care about an airplane — don't they know that his old passion and dream are dead? Since August 2 he has not given them a

thought. However, he begins a conversation with
the pilot, who is a sergeant. And all at once a new
idea takes possession of him; the old passion re-
vives again under another form; the dream rises
once more.

"How can one enlist in the aviation corps?"

"Arrange it with the captain; go to Pau."

Georges runs at once to the Villa Delphine. His
parents no longer recognize the step and the face
of the preceding days; he looks like their son again;
he is saved.

"Father, I want to go to Pau to-morrow."

"Why this trip to Pau?"

"To enlist in the aviation corps. Before the war
you wouldn't hear of my being an aviator, but in
war aviation is no longer a sport."

"In war — yes, it is certainly quite another
thing."

Next day he reached Pau, where Captain Ber-
nard-Thierry was in command of the aviation
camp. He forced his way through Captain Bernard-
Thierry's door, over the expostulations of the sen-
tries. He explained his case and pleaded his cause
with such fire in his eyes that the officer was dazed
and fascinated. From the tones of the captain's
voice, when he referred to the two successive rejec-
tions, Guynemer knew he had made an impression.
As he had done at Stanislas when he wanted to
soften some punishment inflicted by his master, so
now he brought every argument to bear, one after
another; but with how much more ardor he made
this plea, for his future was at stake! He bewitched

his hearer. And then suddenly he became a child again, imploring and ready to cry.

"Captain, help me — employ me — employ me at anything, no matter what. Let me clean those airplanes over there. You are my last resource. It must be through you that I can do something at last in the war."

The captain reflected gravely. He felt the power hidden in this fragile body. He could not rebuff a suppliant like this one.

"I can take you as student mechanician."

"That's it, that's it; I understand automobiles."

Guynemer exulted, as Jean Krebs' technical lessons flashed already into his mind; they would be of great help in his work. The officer gave him a letter to the recruiting officer at Bayonne, and he went back there for the third time. This time his name was entered, he was taken, and he signed a voluntary engagement. This was on November 21, 1914. There was no need for him to explain to the family what had occurred when he returned to the Villa Delphine: he was beaming.

"You are going?" said his mother and sisters.

"Surely."

Next day he made his *début* at the aviation camp at Pau as student mechanician. He had entered the army by the back door, but he had got in. The future knight of the air was now the humblest of grooms. "I do not ask any favors for him," his father wrote to the captain. "All I ask is that he may perform any services he is capable of." He had to be tried and proved deserving, to pass through all the minor ranks before being worthy to wear the *casque sacré*. The petted child of Compiègne and the Villa Delphine had the most severe of apprenticeships. He slept on the floor, and was employed in the dirtiest work about camp, cleaned cylinders and carried cans of petroleum. In this *milieu* he heard words and theories which dumbfounded him, not knowing then that men frequently do not mean all that they say. On November 26, he wrote Abbé Chesnais: "I have the pleasure of informing you that after two postponements during a vain effort to enlist, I have at last succeeded. *Time and patience* . . . I am writing you in the mess, while two comrades are elaborating social theories. . . ."

Would he be able to endure this workman's existence? His parents were not without anxiety. They hesitated to leave Biarritz and return to their home in Compiègne in the rue Saint-Lazare, on the edge of the forest. But, so far from being injured by manual labor, the child constantly grew stronger. In his case spirit had always triumphed over matter, and compelled it to obedience on every occasion. So now he followed his own object with indomitable energy. He took an airplane to pieces before mounting in it, and learned to know it in every detail.

His preparation for the École Polytechnique assured him a brilliant superiority in his present surroundings. He could explain the laws of mechanics, and tell his wonderstruck comrades what is meant by the resultant of several forces and the equilibrium of forces, giving them unexpected

notions about kinematics and dynamics.[1] From
the laboratory or industrial experiments then being
made, he acquired, on his part, a knowledge of the
resisting power of the materials used in aviation:
wood, steel, steel wires, aluminum and its com-
posites, copper, copper alloys and tissues. He saw
things made — those famous wings that were one
day to carry him up into the blue — with their
longitudinal spars of ash or hickory, their ribs of
light wood, their interior bracing of piano wire,
their other bracing wires, and their wing cover-
ing. He saw the workmen prepare all the material
for mortise and tenon work, saw them attach the
tension wires, fit in the ends of poles, and finally
connect together all the parts of an airplane, —
wings, rudders, motor, landing frame, body. As a
painter grinds his colors before making use of them,
so Guynemer's prelude to his future flights was to
touch with his hands — those long white hands of
the rich student, now tanned and callous, often
coated with soot or grease, and worthy to be the
hands of a laborer — every piece, every bolt and
screw of these machines which were to release him
from his voluntary servitude.

One of his future comrades, *sous-lieutenant* Mar-
cel Viallet (who one day had the honor of bringing
down two German airplanes in ten minutes with
seven bullets), thus describes him at the Pau
school: "I had already had my attention drawn

[1] See *Étude raisonnée de l'aéroplane*, by Jules Bordeaux,
formerly student at École Polytechnique (Gauthier-Billars,
edition 1912).

to this 'little girl' dressed in a private's uniform whom one met in the camp, his hands covered with castor oil, his face all stains, his clothes torn. I do not know what he did in the workshop, but he certainly did not add to its brilliance by his appearance. We saw him all the time hanging around the 'zincs.' His highly interested little face amused us. When we landed, he watched us with such admiration and envy! He asked us endless questions and constantly wanted explanations. Without seeming to do so, he was learning. For a reply to some question about the art of flying, he would have run to the other end of the camp to get us a few drops of gasoline for our tanks. . . ." [1]

He was learning, and when he saw his way clear, he wanted to begin flying. New Year's Day arrived — that sad New Year's Day of the first year of the war. What gifts would he ask of his father? He would ask for help to win his diploma as pilot. "Don't you know somebody in your class at Saint-Cyr who could help me?" He always associated his father with every step he took in advance. The child had no fear of creating a conflict between his father's love for him and the service due to France: he knew very well that he would never receive from his father any counsel against his honor, and without pity he compelled him to facilitate his son's progress toward mortal danger. Certain former classmates of M. Guynemer's at Saint-Cyr had, in fact, reached the rank of general, and the influence of one of them hastened Guynemer's

[1] *Le Petit Parisien*, September 27, 1917.

promotion from student mechanician to student pilot (January 26, 1915).

On this same date, Guynemer, soldier of the 2d Class, began his first journal of flights. The first page is as follows:

Wednesday, January 27: Doing camp chores.
Thursday, " 28: ib.
Friday, " 29: Lecture and camp chores.
Saturday, " 30: Lecture at the Blériot aërodrome.
Sunday, " 31: ib. aërodrome.
Monday, February 1: Went out twenty minutes on Blériot "roller."

The Blériot "roller," called the Penguin because of its abbreviated wings, and which did not leave the ground, was followed on Wednesday, February 17, by a three-cylinder 25 H.P. Blériot, which rose only thirty or forty meters. These were the first ascensions before launching into space. Then came a six-cylinder Blériot, and ascensions became more numerous. Finally, on Wednesday, March 10, the journal records two flights of twenty minutes each on a Blériot six-cylinder 50 H.P., one at a height of 600 meters, the other at 800, with tacking and volplaning descents. This time the child sailed into the sky. Guynemer's first flight, then, was on March 10, 1915.

This journal, with its fifty pages, ends on July 28, 1916, with the following statement:

Friday, July 28. — Round at the front. Attacked a group of four enemy airplanes and forced down one of them. Attacked a second group of four airplanes, which immediately dispersed. Chased one of the airplanes and fired about 250 cartridges: the Boche dived, and seemed to be hit. When I shot the last cartridges from the Vickers, one blade of the screw was perforated with bullet-holes, the dislocated motor struck the machine violently and seriously injured it. Volplaned down to the aërodrome of Chipilly without accident.

A marginal note states that the aëroplane which "seemed to be hit" was brought down, and that the English staff confirmed its fall. This victory of July 28, 1916, on the Somme, was Guynemer's eleventh; and at that time he had flown altogether 348 hours, 25 minutes. This journal of fifty pages enables us to measure the distance covered.

Impassioned young people! You who in every department of achievement desire to win the trophies of a Guynemer, never forget that your progress on the path to glory begins with "doing chores."

CANTO II
LAUNCHED INTO SPACE

I. THE FIRST VICTORY

THE apprentice pilot, then, left the ground for the first time at the Pau school on February 17, 1915, in a three-cylinder Blériot. But these were only short leaps, though sufficiently audacious ones. His monitor accused him of breakneck recklessness: "Too much confidence, madness, fantastical humor." That same evening he wrote describing his impressions to his father: "Before departure, a bit worried; in the air, wildly amusing. When the machine slid or oscillated I was not at all troubled, it even seemed funny.... Well, it diverted me immensely, but it was lucky that *Maman* was not there.... I don't think I have achieved a reputation for prudence. I hope everything will go well; I shall soon know...."

During February he made many experimental flights, and finally, on March 10, 1915, went up 600 meters. This won him next day a diploma from the Aëro Club, and the day following he wrote to his sister Odette this hymn of joy — not long, but unique in his correspondence: "Uninterrupted descent, volplaning for 800 meters. Superb view (sunset)...."

"Superb view (sunset)": in the hundred and fifty or two hundred letters addressed to his family, I believe this is the only landscape. Slightly later, but infrequently, the new aviator gave a few details of observation, the accuracy of which lent them some picturesqueness; but in this letter he yielded to the intoxication of the air, he enjoyed flying as if it were his right. He experienced that sensation of lightness and freedom which accompanies the separation from earth, the pleasure of cleaving the wind, of controlling his machine, of seeing, breathing, thinking differently from the way he saw and thought and breathed on the land, of being born, in fact, into a new and solitary life in an enlarged world. As he ascended, men suddenly diminished in size. The earth looked as if some giant hand had smoothed its surface, diversified only by moving shadows, while the outlines of objects became stronger, so that they seemed to be cut in relief.

The land was marked by geometrical lines, showing man's labor and its regularity, an immense parti-colored checker-board traversed by the lines of highroads and rivers, and containing islands which were forests and towns and cities. Was it the chain of the Pyrenees covered with snow which, breaking this uniformity, wrested a cry of admiration from the aviator? What shades of gold and purple were shed over the scene by the setting sun? His half-sentence is like a confession of love for the joy of living, violently torn from him, and the only avowal this blunt Roland would allow himself.

For the nature of his correspondence is somewhat
surprising. Read superficially, it must seem extremely monotonous; but when better understood,
it indicates the writer's sense of oppression, of hal-
lucination, of being bewitched. From that moment
Guynemer had only one object, and from its pursuit he never once desisted. Or, if he did desist for
a brief interval, it was only to see his parents, who
were part of his life, and whom he associated with
his work. His correspondence with them is full of
his airplanes, his flights, and then his enemy-
chasing. His letters have no beginning and no
ending, but plunge at once into action. He himself
was nothing but action. Only that? the reader will
ask. Action was his reason for existing, his heart,
his soul — action in which his whole being fas-
tened on his prey.

A long and minutiose training goes to the making of a good pilot. But the impatient Guynemer
had patience for everything, and the self-willed
Stanislas student became the hardest working of
apprentices. His scientific knowledge furnished him
with a method, and after his first long flights his
progress was very rapid. But he wanted to master
all the principles of aviation. As student mechanician he had seen airplanes built. He intended to
make himself veritably part of the machine which
should be intrusted to him. Each of his senses was
to receive the education which, little by little,
would make it an instrument capable of registering
facts and effecting security. His eyes — those
piercing eyes which were to excel in raking the

heavens and perceiving the first trace of an enemy at incalculable distances — though they could only register his motion in relation to the earth and not the air, could, at all events, inform him of the slightest deviations from the horizontal in the three dimensions: namely, straightness of direction, lateral and longitudinal horizontality, and accurately appreciate angular variations. When the motor slowed up or stopped, his ear would interpret the sound made by the wind on the piano wires, the tension wires, the struts and canvas; while his touch, still more sure, would know by the degree of resistance of the controlling elements the speed action of the machine, and his skillful hands would prepare the work of death. "In the case of the bird," says the *Manual*, by M. Maurice Percheron, "its feathers connect its organs of stability with the brain; while the experienced aviator has his controlling elements which produce the movement he wishes, and inform him of the disturbing motions of the wind." But with Guynemer the movements he wanted were never brought about as the result of reflex nervous action. At no time, even in the greatest danger, did he ever cease to govern every maneuver of his machine by his own thought. His rapidity of conception and decision was astounding, but was never mere instinct. As pilot, as hunter, as warrior, Guynemer invariably controlled his airplane and his gun with his brain. This is why his apprenticeship was so important, and why he himself attached so much importance to it — by instinct, in this case. His nerves were always strained, but he worked out his results. Behind every action was the power of his will, that power which had forced his entrance into the army, and itself closed the doors behind him, a prisoner of his own vocation.

He familiarized himself with all the levers of the engine and every part of the controlling elements. When the obligatory exercises were finished, and his comrades were resting and idling, he remounted the airplane, as a child gets onto his rocking-horse, and took the levers again into his hands: When he went up, he watched for the exact instant for quitting the ground and sought the easiest line of ascension; during flights, he was careful about his position, avoiding too much diving, or nosing-up, maintaining a horizontal movement, making sure of his lateral and longitudinal equilibrium, familiarizing himself with winds, and adapting his motions to every sort of rocking. When he came down, and the earth seemed to leap up at him, he noted the angle and swiftness of the descent and found the right height at which to slow down. Although his first efforts had been so clever that his monitors were convinced for a long time that he had already been a pilot, yet it is not so much his talent that we should admire as his determination. He was more successful than others because he wore himself out during the whole of his short life in trying to do better — to do better in order to serve better. He worked more than any one else; when he was not satisfied with himself he began all over again, and sought the cause of his errors. There are many other pilots as gifted as Guynemer, but he possessed an energy which was extraordinary, and in this respect excelled all the rest.

And there were no limits to the exercise of this energy. He gave his own body to complete so to speak, the airplane, — a centaur of the air. The wind that whistled through his tension wires and canvas made his own body vibrate like the piano wires. His body was so sensitive that it, too, seemed to obey the rudder. Nothing that concerned his voyages was either unknown or negligible to him. He verified all his instruments — the map-holder, the compass, the altimeter, the tachometer, the speedometer — with searching care. Before every flight he himself made sure that his machine was in perfect condition. When it was brought out of the hangar he looked it over as they look over race-horses, and never forgot this task. How would it be when he should have his own airplane?

At Pau he increased the number of his flights, and changed airplanes, leaving the Blériot Gnome for the Morane. His altitudes at this time varied from 500 to 600 meters. Going, on March 21, to the Avord school, he went up on the 28th to a height of 1500 meters, and on April 1 to 2600. His flights became longer, and lasted one hour, then an hour and a half. The spiral descent from a height of 500 meters, with the motor switched off, tri-angular voyages, the test of altitude and that of duration of flight, which were necessary for his military diploma, soon became nothing more to

him than sport. In May nearly every day he piloted
one passenger on an M.S.P. (Morane-Saunier-
Parasol). During all this period his record-book
registers only one breakdown. Finally, on May 25,
he was sent to the general Aviation Reserves, and
on the 31st made two flights in a Nieuport with
a passenger. This was the end of his apprenticeship,
and on June 8 Corporal Georges Guynemer was
designated as member of Escadrille M. S. 3, which
he joined next day at Vauciennes.

This M. S. 3 was the future N. 3, the "Ciogog-
nes" or Storks Escadrille. It was already commanded by Captain Brocard, under whose orders
it was destined to become illustrious. Védrines belonged to it. *Sous-lieutenant de cavalerie* Deullin
joined it almost simultaneously with Guynemer,
whose friend he soon became. Later, little by little,
came Heurtaux, de la Tour, Dorme, Auger, Raymond, etc., all the famous valiant knights of the
escadrille, like the peers of France who followed
Roland over the Spanish roads. This aviation camp
was at Vauciennes, near Villers-Cotterets, in the
Valois country with its beautiful forests, its cha-
teaux, its fertile meadows, and its delicate outlines made shadowy by the humid vapor rising
from ponds or woods. "Complete calm," wrote
Guynemer on June 9, "not one sound of any kind;
one might think oneself in the Midi, except that
the inhabitants have seen the beast at close
range, and know how to appreciate us. . . . Védrines
is very friendly and has given me excellent advice.
He has recommended me to his '*mecanos*,' who

are the real type of the clever Parisian, inventive, lively and good humored. ...." Next day he gives some details of his billet, and adds: "I have had a *mitrailleuse* support mounted on my machine, and now I am ready for the hunt. ... Yesterday at five o'clock I darted around above the house at 1700 or 2000 meters. Did you see me? I forced my motor for five minutes in hopes that you would hear me." He had recently parted from his family, and a happy chance had brought him to fight over the very lines that protected his own home. The front of the Sixth Army to which he was attached, extending from Ribécourt beyond the forest of Laigue, passed in front of Railly and Tracy-le-Val, hollowed itself before the enemy salient of Moulin-sous-Touvent, straightened itself again near Autrèches and Nouvron-Vingré, covered Soissons, whose very outskirts were menaced, was obliged to turn back on the left bank of the Aisne where the enemy took, in January, 1915, the bridge-head at Condé, and Vailly and Chavonne, and crossed the river again at Soupir which belonged to us. Laon, La Fère, Coucy-le-Château, Chauny, Noyon, Ham, and Péronne were the objects of his reconnoitering flights.

War acts more poignantly, more directly upon a soldier whose own home is immediately behind him. If the front were pierced in the sector which had been intrusted to him, his own people would be exposed. So he becomes their sentinel. Under such conditions, *la Patrie* is no longer merely the historic soil of the French people, the sacred ground every

parcel of which is responsible for all the rest, but
also the beloved home of infancy, the home of
parents, and, for this collegian of yesterday, the
scene of charming walks and delightful vacations.
He has but just now left the paternal mansion;
and, not yet accustomed to the separation, he
visits it by the roads of the air, the only ones which
he is now free to travel. He does not take advantage
of his proximity to Compiègne to go ring the familiar door-bell, because he is a soldier and respects
orders; but, on returning from his rounds, he does
not hesitate to turn aside a bit in order to pass
over his home, indulging up there in the sky in
all sorts of acrobatic caprioles to attract attention
and prolong the interview. What lover was ever
more ingenious and madder in his rendezvous?

Throughout all his correspondence he recalls
his air visits. "You must have seen my head, for
I never took my eyes off the house. . . ." Or, after
an aërial somersault that filled all those down
below with terror: "I am wretched to know that
my veering the other day frightened *maman* so
much, but I did it so as to see the house without
having to lean over the side of the machine, which
is unpleasant on account of the wind. . . ." Or
sometimes he threw down a paper which was
picked up in Count Foy's park: "Everything is
all right." He thought he was reassuring his
parents about his safety; but their state of mind
can be conceived when they beheld, exactly over
their heads, an airplane engaged apparently in
performing a dance, while through their binocu-

lars they could see the tiny black speck of a head which looked over its side. He had indeed a singular fashion of reassuring them!

Meanwhile, at Vauciennes the newcomer was being tested. At first he was thought to look rather sickly and weak, to be somewhat reserved and distant, and too well dressed, with a "young-ladyish" air. He was known to be already an expert pilot, capable of making tail spins after barely three months' experience. But still the men felt some uncertainty about this youngster whom they dared not trifle with on account of his eyes, "out of which fire and spirit flowed like a torrent." [1] Later on they were to know him better.

A legend was current as to the large quantity of "wood broken" by Guynemer in his early days with the escadrille. This is radically untrue, and his notebook contradicts it. From the very first day the *débutant* fulfilled the promise of his apprentice days. After one or two trial flights, he left for a scouting expedition on Sunday, June 13, above the enemy lines, and there met three German airplanes. On the 14th he described what he had seen in a letter to his father. — His correspondence still included some description at that time, the earth still held his attention; but it was soon to lose interest for him. — "The appearance of Tracy and Quennevières," he wrote, "is simply unbelievable: ruins, an inextricable entanglement of trenches almost touching one another, the soil turned over by the shells, the holes of which one

[1] Saint-Simon.

sees by thousands. One wonders how there could be a single living man there. Only a few trees of a wood are left standing, the others beaten down by the "*marmites*," [1] and everywhere may be seen the yellow color of the literally plowed-up earth. It seems incredible that all these details can be seen from a height of over 3000 meters. I could see to a distance of 60 or 70 kilometers, and never lost sight of Compiègne. Saint-Quentin, Péronne, etc., were as distinct as if I were there. . . ."

Next day, the 14th, another reconnaissance, of which the itinerary was Coucy, Laon, La Fère, Tergnier, Appily, Vic-sur-Aisne. Not a cannon shot disturbed these first two expeditions. But danger lurked under this apparent security, and on the 15th he was saluted by shells, dropping quite near. It was his "baptism by fire," and only inspired this sentence *à la Duguesclin:* "No impression, except satisfied curiosity."

The following days were passed in a perfect tempest, and he only laughed. The new Roland, the bold and marvelous knight, is already revealed in the letters to be given below. On the 16th he departed on his rounds, carrying, as observer, Lieutenant de Lavalette. His airplane was hit by a shell projectile in the right wing. On the 17th his machine returned with eight wounds, two in the right wing, four in the body, and in addition one strut and one longitudinal spar hit. On the 18th he returned from a reconnaissance with Lieutenant Colcomb during which his machine

[1] Shells.

had been hit in the right wing, the rudder, and the body. But his notebook only contains statements of facts, and we have to turn to his correspondence for more details.

"Decidedly," he wrote on June 17 to his sister Odette, "the Boches have quite a special affection for me, and the parts of my '*coucou*' serve me for a calendar. Yesterday we flew over Chauny, Tergnier, Laon, Coucy, Soissons. Up to Chauny my observer had counted 243 shells; Coucy shot 500 to 600; my observer estimated 1000 shots in all. All we heard was a rolling sound, and then the shells burst everywhere, below us, above, in front, behind, on the right and on the left, for we descended to take some photographs of a place which they did not want us to see. We could hear the shell-fragments whistling past; there was one that, after piercing the wing, passed within the radius of the propeller without touching it, and then to within fifty centimeters of my face; another entered by the same hole but stayed there, and I will send it to you. Fragments also struck the rudder, and one the body." (His journal mentions more.) "My observer, who has been an observer from the beginning, says that he never saw a cannonade like that one, and that he was glad to get back again. At one moment a bomb-head of 105 millimeters, which we knew by its shape and the color of its explosion, fell on us and just grazed us. In fact, we often see enormous shells exploding. It is very curious. On our return we met Captain Gerard, and my observer told him that I

had astounding nerve; *zim, boum boum!* He said
he knew it. . . . I will send you a photograph of my
'*coucou*' with its nine bruises: it is superb."

The next day, June 18, it was his mother who
received his confidences. The enemy had bombarded Villers-Cotterets with a long-distance gun
which had to be discovered. On this occasion he
took Lieutenant Colcomb as observer: "At Coucy,
terribly accurate cannonade: *toc, toc,* two projectiles in the right wing, one within a meter of me;
we went on with our observations in the same
place. Suddenly a formidable crash: a shell burst
8 to 10 meters under the machine. Result: three
holes, one strut and one spar spoiled. We went on
for five minutes longer observing the same spot,
always encircled, naturally. Returning, the shooting was less accurate. On landing, my observer
congratulated me for not having moved or zig-
zagged, which would have bothered his observation.
We had, in fact, only made very slight and very
slow changes of altitude, speed, and direction.
Compliments from him mean something, for
nobody has better nerve. In the evening Captain
Gerard, in command of army aviation, called me
and said: 'You are a nervy pilot, all right; you
won't spoil our reputation by lack of pluck —
quite the contrary. For a beginner! —' and he
asked me how long I had been a corporal. *Y a bon.*
My '*coucou*' is superb, with its parts all dated in
red. You can see them all, for those underneath
spread up over the sides. In the air I showed each
hole in the wing, as it was hit, to the passenger,

and he was enchanted, too. It's a thrilling sport.
It is a bore, though, when they burst over our
heads, because I cannot see them, though I can
hear. The observer has to give me information in
that case. Just now, *le roi n'est pas mon cousin.* ...."

Lieutenant, now Captain, Colcomb, has completed this account. During the entire period of his
observation, the pilot, in fact, did not make any
maneuver or in any way shake the machine in
order to dodge the firing. He simply sent the airplane a bit higher and calmly lowered it again
over the spot to be photographed, as if he were
master of the air. The following dialogue occurred:

The Observer: "I have finished; we can go back."

The Pilot: "Lieutenant, do me the favor of
photographing for me the projectiles falling around
us."

Children have always had a passion for pictures;
and the pictures were taken.

The chasers and bombardiers in the history of
aviation have attracted public attention to the
detriment of their comrades, the observers, whose
admirable services will become better known in
time. It is by them that the battle field is exposed,
and the preparations and ruses of the enemy
balked: they are the eyes of the commanders, and
also the friends of the troops. On April 29, 1916,
Lieutenant Robbe flew over the trenches of the
Mort-Homme at 200 meters, and brought back a
detailed exposition of the entanglement of the
lines. A year later, in nearly the same place, Lieutenant Pierre Guilland, observer on board a

biplane of the Moroccan division, was forced down by three enemy airplanes just at the moment when his division, whose progress he was following in order to report it, started its attack on the Corbeaux Woods east of the Mort-Homme, on August 20, 1917. He fell on the first advancing lines and was picked up, unconscious and mortally wounded, by an artillery officer who proceeded to carry out the aviator's mission. When the latter reopened his eyes — for only a short while — he asked: "Where am I?" — "North of Chattancourt, west of Cumières." — "Has the attack succeeded?" — "Every object has been attained." — "Ah! that's good, that's good." ... He made them repeat the news to him. He was dying, but his division was victorious.

Near Frise, Lieutenant Sains, who had been obliged to land on July 1, 1916, was rescued by the French army on July 4, after having hidden himself for three days in a shell-hole to avoid surrendering, his pilot, Quartermaster de Kyspotter, having been killed.

During the battle of the Aisne in April, 1917, Lieutenant Godillot, whose pilot had also been killed, slid along the plane, sat on the knees of the dead pilot, and brought the machine back into the French lines. And Captain Méry, Lieutenant Viguier, Lieutenant de Saint-Séverin, and Fressagues, Floret, de Niort, and Major Challe, Lieutenant Boudereau, Captain Roeckel, and Adjutant Fonck — who was to become famous as a chaser — how many of these élite observers fur-

thered the destruction wrought by the artillery,
and aided the progress of the infantry!

On October 24, 1916, as the fog cleared away,
I saw the airplane of the Guyot de Salins division
fly over Fort Douaumont just at the moment when
Major Nicolai's marines entered there.[1] The airplane had descended so low into the mist that it
seemed as if magnetically drawn down by the
earth, and the observer, leaning over the edge,
was clapping his hands to applaud the triumph of
his comrades. The latter saw his gesture, even
though they could not hear the applause, and
cheered him — a spontaneous exchange of soldierly
confidence and affection between the sky and the
earth.

Almost exactly one year later, on October 23,
1917, I saw the airplane of the same division
hovering over the Fort of the Malmaison just as
the Giraud batallion of the 4th Zouaves Regiment
took possession of it. At dawn it came to observe
and note the site of the commanding officer's post,
and to read the optical signals announcing our
success. At each visit it seemed like the moving
star of old, now guiding the new shepherds, the
guardians of our dear human flocks — not over
the stable where a God was born, but over the
ruins where victory was born.

Later on Captain Colcomb spoke of Guynemer
as "the most sublime military figure I have ever
been permitted to behold, one of the finest and

[1] See *Les Captifs délivrés*.

THE FIRST FLIGHT IN A BLÉRIOT

most generous souls I have ever known." Guynemer was not satisfied to be merely calm and systematically immovable, and to display sang-froid, though to an extraordinary degree. He amused himself by counting the holes in his wings, and pointing them out to the observer. He was furious when the explosions occurred outside his range of vision, because he was not resigned to missing anything. He seemed to juggle with the shrapnel. And after landing, he rushed off to his escadrille chief, Captain Brocard, took him by the arm, and never left him until he had drawn him almost by force to his machine, compelling him to put his fingers into the wounds, exulting meanwhile and fairly bounding with joy. Captain, now Major Brocard, felt quite sure of him from that time, and referred to him later in these words: "Very young: his extraordinary self-confidence and natural qualities will very soon make him an excellent pilot. . . ."

His curiosity, indeed, was satisfied; and to whom would he confide all the risks that he ran? His mother and his sisters, the hearts which were the most troubled about him, and whose peace and happiness he had carried off into the air. He never dreamed of the torment he caused them, and which they knew how to conceal from him. Even the idea of such a thing never occurred to him. As they loved him, they loved him just as he was, in the raw. He was too young to dissimulate, too young to spare them. He knew nothing either of lies or of pity. He never thought that any one could suffer anguish about a son or a brother when this son and brother was himself supremely happy in his vocation. He was naïvely cruel.

But the rounds and reconnaissances were not to hold him long; and he already scented other adventures. He had scented the odor of the beast, and he had his airplane furnished with a support for a machine-gun. That particular airplane, it is true, came to an untimely end in a ditch, but was already condemned by its body-frame, which was rotten with bullet holes. That was the only "wood" Guynemer "broke" during his early flights.

But his next airplane was also armed, and in the young pilot could already be plainly seen that taste for enemy-chasing which was to bewitch and take possession of him. Though after this time he certainly carried over the lines Lieutenant de Lavalette, Lieutenant Colcomb and Captain Siméon, and always with equal calm, yet he aspired to other flights, further away from earth. Lieutenant de Beauchamp — the future Captain de Beauchamp, who was to die so soon after his audacious raids on Essen and Munich — divined what was hidden in this thin boy who was in such breathless haste to get on. He would not allow Corporal Guynemer to address him as lieutenant, feeling so surely his equality, and to-morrow perhaps his mastery. On July 6, 1915, he sent him a little guide for aviators in a few lines: "Be cautious. Look well at what is happening around you before acting. Invoke Saint Benoît every morning. But above all, write in letters of fire in your memory:

In aviation, everything not useful should be avoided."
Oh, of course! The "little girl" laughed at the
advice as he laughed at the tempest. He had an
admiration for Beauchamp, but when did a Roland
ever listen to an Oliver? One day he went up in a
wind of over 25 meters, and even by nosing-up
a bit he could hardly make any progress. With the
wind behind him he made over 200 kilometers.
Then he landed. Védrines addressed a few warning
remarks to him, and he was thought to be calmed.
But off he went again before the frightened spec-
tators. He would always do too much, and nothing
could restrain him.

The importance of the development of aviation
in the war had been foreseen neither by the Germans nor ourselves. If before the beginning of
the campaign the military chiefs had understood
all the services which would be rendered by aërial
strategic scouting, the regulation of artillery fire
would not have still been in an experimental
stage. No one knew the help which was to be de-
rived from aërial photography. The air duel was
regarded simply as a possible incident that might
occur during a patrol or a reconnaissance, and in
view of which the observer or mechanician armed
himself with a gun or an automatic pistol. Airplanes armed with machine-guns were very
exceptional, and at the end of 1914 there were only
thirty. The Germans used them generally before
we did; but it was the French aviators, nevertheless, who forced the Germans to fight in the air.
I had the opportunity in October, 1914, to see,

from a hill on the Aisne, one of these first airplane combats, which ended by the enemy falling on the outskirts of the village of Muizon on the left bank of the Vesle. The French champion bore the fine name of Franc, and piloted a Voisin. At that date it was not unusual to pick up messages dropped within our lines by enemy pilots, substantially to this effect: "Useless for us to fight each other; there are enough risks without that. . . ."

Meanwhile, strategic reconnaissance was perfected as the line of the front became firmly established, and more and more importance was accorded to the search for objectives. Remarkable results were attained by air photography from December, 1914; and after January, 1915, the regulation of artillery fire by wireless telegraphy was in general practice. It was necessary to protect the airplanes attached to army corps, and to clean up the air for their free circulation. This rôle devolved upon the most rapid airplanes, which were then the Morane-Saunier-Parasols, and in the spring of 1915 these formed the first *escadrilles de chasse*, one for each army. Garros, already popular before the war for having been the first air-pilot to cross the Mediterranean, from Saint-Raphael to Bizerto, forced down a large Aviatik above Dixmude in April, 1915. A few days later a motor breakdown compelled him to land at Ingelminster, north of Courtrai, and he was made prisoner.[1] The aviators, like the knights of ancient

[1] The romantic circumstances under which he escaped in February, 1918, are well known.

times, sent one another challenges. Sergeant David
— who was killed shortly after — having been
obliged to refuse to fight an enemy airplane because his machine-gun jammed, dropped a challenge to the latter on the German aërodrome, and
waited at the place, on the day and hour fixed,
at Vauquois (noon, in June, 1915, above the German lines), but his adversary never came to the
rendezvous.

The Maurice Farman and Caudron airplanes
were used for observation. The Voisin machines,
strong but slower, were more especially utilized
for bombardments, which began to be carried out
by organized expeditions. The famous raids on the
Ludwigshafen factories and the Karlsruhe railway
station occurred in June, 1915. It was at the battle
of Artois (May and June, 1915) that aviation for
the first time constituted a branch of the army;
and the work was chiefly done by the escadrilles
belonging to the army corps, which rendered very
considerable services as scouts and in aërial
photography and destructive fire. But as an enemy
chaser, the airplane was still regarded with much
distrust and incredulity. Some said it was useless;
was it not sufficient that the airplanes of the army
corps and those for bombardments could defend
themselves? Others of less extreme opinions thought
it should be limited to the part of protector. This
opposition was overcome by the sudden development of the German enemy-chasing airplanes after
July, 1915, subsequent to our raids on Ludwigshafen
and Karlsruhe, which aroused furious anger in
Germany.

In the beginning the belligerent nations had collected the most heterogeneous group of all the airplane models then available. But the methodical Germans, without delay, supplied their constructors with definite types of machines in order to make their escadrilles harmonious. At that time they used monoplanes for reconnaissances, without any special arrangement for carrying arms, and incapable of carrying heavy weights; and biplanes for observation, unarmed, and possessing only a makeshift contrivance for launching bombs. The machines of both these series were two-seated, with the passenger in front. These were Albatros, Aviatiks, Eulers, Rumplers, and Gothas. Early in 1915 appeared the Fokkers, which were one-seated, and new two-seated machines, Aviatiks or Albatros, which were more rapid, with the passenger at the rear, and furnished with a revolving turret for the machine-gun. The German troops engaged in aërostation, aviation, automobile and railway service were grouped as communication troops (*Verkehrstruppen*), under the direction of the General Inspection of Military Communications. It was not until the autumn of 1916 that the aërostation, aviation, and aërial defense troops were made independent and, under the title of *Luftstreitkrafte* (aërial combatant forces), took their position in the order of battle between the pioneers and the communication troops. But early in the summer of 1915 the progress realized in aviation resulted in its forming a separate branch of the army, with campaign and enemy-chasing escadrilles.

Guynemer was now on the straight road toward aërial combat. Most of our pilots were still chasing enemy airplanes with one passenger armed with a simple musketoon. More circumspect than the others, Guynemer had his airplane armed with a machine-gun. Meanwhile the staff was preparing to reorganize the army escadrilles. The bold Pégoud had several times fought with too enterprising Fokkers or Aviatiks; Captain Brocard had forced down one of them in flames over Soissons; and the latest recruit of the escadrille, this youngster of a Guynemer, was burning to have his own Boche.

The first entries in his notebook of flights for July, 1915, record expeditions without result, in company with Adjutant Hatin, Lieutenant de Ruppiere, in the region of Noyon, Roye, Ham, and Coucy-le-Château. On the 10th, the *chasseurs* put to flight three Albatros, while a more rapid Fokker attempted an attack, but turned back having tried a shot at their machine-gun. On the 16th Guynemer and Hatin dropped bombs on the Chauny railway station; during the bombardment an Aviatik attacked them, they stood his fire, replying as well as they could with their musketoon, and returned to camp uninjured. Adjutant Hatin was decorated with the Military Medal. As Hatin was a *gourmet*, Guynemer went that same evening to Le Bourget to fetch two bottles of Rhine wine to celebrate this family fête. At Le Bourget he tried the new Nieuport machine, which was the hope of the fighting airplanes. Finally, on July 19

— memorable date — his journal records Guynemer's first victory:

"Started with Guerder after a Boche reported
at Couvres and caught up with him over Pierre-
fonds. Shot one belt, machine-gun jammed, then
unjammed. The Boche fled and landed in the
direction of Laon. At Coucy we turned back and
saw an Aviatik going toward Soissons at about
3200 meters up. We followed him, and as soon as
he was within our lines we dived and placed ourselves about 50 meters under and behind him at the
left. At our first salvo, the Aviatik lurched, and
we saw a part of the machine crack. He replied
with a rifle shot, one ball hitting a wing, another
grazing Guerder's hand and head. At our last shot
the pilot sank down on the body-frame, the observer raised his arms, and the Aviatik fell straight
downward in flames, between the trenches. . . ."

This flight began at 3700 meters in the air, and
lasted ten minutes, the two combatants being
separated by a distance of 50 and sometimes 20
meters. The statement of fact is characteristic of
Guynemer. An unforgettable sight had been imprinted on his eyes: the pilot sinking down in his
cock-pit, the arms of the observer beating the air,
the burning airplane sinking. Such were to be his
future landscape sketches, done in the sky. The
wings of the bird of prey were unfurled definitely
in space.

The two fighting airmen had left Vauciennes at
two o'clock in the afternoon, and at quarter-past
three they landed, conquerors, at Carrière l'Evêque.

From their opposing camps the infantry had followed the fight with their eyes. The Germans, made furious by defeat, cannonaded the landing-place. Georges, who was too thin for his clothes, and whose leather pantaloons lined with sheepskin, which he wore over his breeches, slipped and impeded his walking, sat down under the exploding shells and calmly took them off. Then he placed the machine in a position of greater safety, but broke the propeller on a pile of hay. During this time a crowd had come running and now surrounded the victors. Artillery officers escorted them off, sentinels saluted them, a colonel offered them champagne. Guerder was taken first into the commanding officer's post, and on being questioned about the maneuver that won the victory excused himself with modesty:

"That was the pilot's affair."

Guynemer, who had stolen in, was willing to talk.

"Who is this?" asked the colonel.

"That's the pilot."

"You? How old are you?"

"Twenty."

"And the gunner?"

"Twenty-two."

"The deuce! There are nothing but children left to do the fighting."

So, passed along in this manner from staff to staff, they finally landed at Compiègne, conducted by Captain Siméon. No happiness was complete for Guynemer if his home was not associated with it.

"He will get the Military Medal," declared Captain Siméon, "because he wanted his Boche and went after him."

Words of a true chief who knew his men. Always to go after what he wanted was the basic characteristic of Guynemer. And now various details concerning the combat came one by one to light. Guerder had been half out of the machine to have the machine-gun ready to hand. When the gun jammed, Georges yelled to his comrade how to release it. Guerder, who had picked up his rifle, laid it down, executed the maneuver indicated by Guynemer, and resumed his machine-gun fire. This episode lasted two minutes during which Georges maintained the airplane under the Aviatik, unwilling to change his position, as he saw that a recoil would expose them to the Boche's gun.

Meanwhile Védrines came in search of the victor, and piloted the machine back to headquarters, with Guynemer on board seated on the body and quivering with joy.

With this very first victory Guynemer sealed his friendship with the infantry, whom his youthful audacity had comforted in their trenches. He received the following letter, dated July 20, 1915:

Lieutenant-colonel Maillard, commanding the 238th Infantry, to Corporal Pilot Guynemer and Mechanician Guerder of Escadrille M.S. 3, at Vauciennes.

The Lieutenant-colonel,
The Officers,
The whole Regiment,

Having witnessed the aërial attack you made upon
a German Aviatik over their trenches, spontaneously
applauded your victory which terminated in the vertical
fall of your adversary. They offer you their warmest
congratulations, and share the joy you must have felt
in achieving so brilliant a success.   MAILLARD.

On July 21 the Military Medal was given to the
two victors, Guynemer's being accompanied by the
following mention: "Corporal Guynemer: a pilot
full of spirit and audacity, volunteering for the
most dangerous missions. After a hot pursuit, gave
battle to a German airplane, which ended in the
burning and destruction of the latter." The
decoration was bestowed on August 4 at Vauciennes by General Dubois, then in command of
the Sixth Army, and in presence of his father, who
had been sent for. Then Guynemer paid for his
newly won glory by a few days of fever.

II. FROM THE AISNE TO VERDUN

Guynemer's first victory occurred on July 19,
1915, and for his second he had to wait nearly six
months. This was not because he had not been on
the watch. He would have been glad to mount a
Nieuport, but, after all, he had had his Boche, and
at that time the exploit was exceptional: he had to
be patient, and give his comrades a chance to do
the same.

When finally he obtained the longed-for Nieuport, he flew sixteen hours in five days, and naturally went to parade himself over Compiègne.

Without this dedication to his home, the machine would never be consecrated.

When the overwork incident to such a life forced him to take a little repose, he wandered back to his home like a soul in pain. It was in vain that his parents and his two sisters — whom he called his "kids" as if he were their elder — exhausted their ingenuity to amuse him. This home he loved so much, which he left so recently, and returned to so happily, bringing with him his young fame, no longer sufficed him. Though he was so comfortable there, yet on clear days the house stifled him. On such days he seemed like a school child caught in some fault: a little more and he would have condemned himself. Then his sister Yvonne, who had understood the situation, made a bargain with him.

"What is it you miss here at home?"

"Something you cannot give me. Or rather, yes, you can give it to me. Promise me you will."

"Surely, if it will make you happy."

"I shall be the happiest of men."

"Then it's granted in advance."

"Very well, this is it: every morning you must examine the weather. If it is bad, you will let me sleep."

"And if it is fine?"

"If it is fine, you will wake me up."

His sister was afraid to ask more, as she guessed how he would use a fine day. As she was silent, he pretended to pout with that cajoling manner he could assume, and which fascinated everybody.

"You won't do it? I could not stay home: *c'est plus fort que moi.*"

"But, I promise."

And to keep him at home until he should be cured, more or less, the young girl opened her window every morning and inspected the sky, secretly hoping to find it thickly covered with clouds.

"Clouds, waiting over there, motionless, on the edge of the horizon, what are you waiting for? Will you stand idle and let me awaken my brother, who is resting?"

The clouds being indifferent, the sleeper had to be awakened. He dressed hastily, with a smile at the transparent sky, and soon reached Vauciennes by automobile, where he called for his machine, mounted, ascended, flew, hunted the enemy, and returned to Compiègne for luncheon.

"And you can leave us like that?" remonstrated his mother. "Why, this is your holiday."

"Yes, the effort to leave is all the greater."

"Well? —"

"I like the effort, *Maman.*"

His Antigone forced herself to keep her bargain with him. The sun never shone above the forest in vain, but nevertheless she detested the sun. What a strange Romeo this boy would have made! Without the least doubt he would have charged Juliet to wake him to go to battle, and would never have forgiven her for confounding the lark and the nightingale.

On his return to the aviation camp, in the ab-

sence of his own longed-for victories, he took
pleasure in describing those of others. He knew
nothing of rivalry or envy. He wrote his sister
Odette the following description of a combat
waged by Captain Brocard, who surprised a Boche
from the rear, approached him to within fifteen
meters without being seen, and, just at the moment
when the enemy pilot turned round his head, sent
him seven cartridges from his machine-gun: "Result: one ball in the ear, and another through the
middle of his chest. You can imagine whether the
fall of the machine was instantaneous or not.
There was nothing left of the pilot but one chin,
one ear, one mouth, a torso and material enough to
reconstitute two arms. As to the "*coucou*" (burned),
nothing was left but the motor and a few bits of
iron. The passenger was emptied out during the
fall. . . ." It cannot be said that he had much
consideration for the nerves of young girls. He
treated them as if they were warriors who could
understand everything relating to battles. He
wrote with the same freedom that Shakespeare's
characters use in speech.

Until the middle of September he piloted two-
seated airplanes, carrying one passenger, either as
observer or combatant. At last he went up in his
one-seated Nieuport, reveling in the intoxication
of being alone, that intoxication well known to
lovers of the mountains and the air. Is it the
sensation of liberty, the freedom from all the
usual material bonds, the feeling of coming into
possession of these deserts of space or ice where the

traveler covers leagues without meeting anybody,
the forgetfulness of all that interferes with one's
own personal object? Such solitaries do not easily
accommodate themselves to company which seems
to them to encroach upon their domain, and steal
a part of their enjoyment. Guynemer never enjoyed
anything so much as these lonely rounds in which
he took possession of the whole sky, and woe to
the enemy who ventured into this immensity,
which was now his park.

On September 29, and October 1, 1915, he was
sent on special missions. These special missions
were generally confided to Védrines, who had
accomplished seven. The time is not yet ripe for
a revelation of their details, but they were particularly dangerous, for it was necessary to land in
occupied territory and return. Guynemer's first
mission required three hours' flying. He ascended
in a storm, just as the countermand arrived owing
to the unfavorable weather. When he descended,
volplaning, at daybreak, with slackened, noiseless
motor, and landed on our invaded territory, his
heart beat fast. Some peasants going to their work
in the fields saw him as he ascended again, and
recognizing the tricolor, showed much surprise,
and then extended their hands to him. This mission won for Sergeant Guynemer — he had been
promoted sergeant shortly before — his second
mention: "Has proved his courage, energy and
sang-froid by accomplishing, as a volunteer, an
important and difficult special mission in stormy
weather." — "This palm is worth while," he

wrote in a letter to his parents, "for the mission
was hard." On his way back an English aviator
shot at him, but on recognizing him signaled elabo-
rate excuses.

Some rather exciting reconnaissances with Captain Siméon — one day over Saint-Quentin they
were attacked by a Fokker and, their machine-gun
refusing to work, they were subjected to two
hundred shots from the enemy at 100 meters, then
at 50 meters, so that they were obliged to dive
into a cloud, with one tire gone — and a few bombardments of railway stations and goods depots
did not assuage his fever for the chase. Nothing
sufficed him but to explore and rake the heavens.
On November 6, 3000 meters above Chaulnes, he
waged an epic combat with an L. V. G. (*Luft-
Verkehr-Gesellschaft*), 150 H. P. Having succeeded
in placing himself three meters under his enemy,
he almost laughed with the surety he felt of forcing
him down, when his machine-gun jammed. He
immediately banked, but he was so near the enemy
that the machines interlocked. Would he fall? A
bit of his canvas was torn off, but the airplane
held its own. As he drew away he saw the enormous
enemy machine-gun aimed at him. A bullet
grazed his head. He dived under the Boche, who
retreated. "All the same," Guynemer added gaily,
"if I ever get into a terrible financial fix and have
to become a cab-driver, I shall have memories
which are far from ordinary: a tire exploding at
3400 meters, an interlocking at 3000 meters. That
rotten Boche only owed his life to a spring being

slightly out of order, as was shown by the autopsy on the machine-gun. For my eighth combat, this was decidedly annoying. . . ."

It was annoying, but what could be done? Nothing, in fact, but return to one's apprenticeship. He was perfectly satisfied with his work as a pilot, but it was necessary to avoid these too frequent jammings which saved the enemy. At Stanislas College Guynemer was known as an excellent shot. He began to practice again with his rifle, and with the machine-gun; above all, he carefully examined every part of this delicate weapon, taking it apart and putting it together, and increasing his practice. He became a gunsmith. And there lies the secret of his genius: he never gave up anything, nor ever acknowledged himself beaten. If he failed, he began all over again, but after having sought the cause of his failure in order to remedy it. When he was asked one day to choose a device for himself, he adopted this, which completely expresses his character: *Faire face*. He always faced everything, not only the enemy, but every object which opposed his progress. His determination compelled success. In the career of Guynemer nothing was left to chance, and everything won by effort, pursuit, and implacable will.

On Sunday, December 5, 1915, as he was making his rounds in the Compiègne region, he saw two airplanes more than 3000 meters above Chauny. As the higher one flew over Bailly he sprang upon it and attacked it: at 50 meters, fifteen shots from his machine-gun; at 20 meters, thirty shots. The

German fell in a tail spin, north of Bailly over against the Bois Carré. Guynemer was sure he had forced him down; but the other airplane was still there. He tacked in order to chase and attack him, but in vain, for his second adversary had fled. And when he tried to discover the spot where the first must have fallen, he failed to find it. This was really too much: was he going to lose his prey? Suddenly he had an idea. He landed in a field near Compiègne. It was Sunday, and just noon, and he knew that his parents would be coming home from mass. He watched for them, and as soon as he perceived his father rushed to him:

"Father, I have lost my Boche."

"You have lost your Boche?"

"Yes, an airplane that I have forced down. I must return to my escadrille, but I don't want to lose him."

"What can I do?"

"Why, look for him and find him. He ought to be near Bailly, towards the Bois Carré."

And he vanished, leaving to his father the task of finding the lost airplane as a partridge is found in a field of lucerne. The military authority kindly lent its aid, and in fact the body of the German pilot was discovered on the edge of the Bois Carré, where it was buried.

This victory was ratified, but a few days later the authorities, failing to find the necessary material proof, refused to give Guynemer credit for it. Ah, the regulations refuse the hunter this game? Guynemer, turning very red, declared: "It doesn't

matter, I will get another." He was always want-
ing another; and in fact he got one four days
later, on December 8. This is the report in his
notebook: "Discovering the strategic line Royne-
Nesle. While descending, saw a German airplane
high, and far within its own lines. As it passed the
lines at Beuvraigne, I cut off its retreat and chased
it. I caught up to it in five minutes, and fired
forty-seven shots from my Lewis from a point 20
meters behind and under it. The enemy airplane,
an L. V. G. 165 H. P. probably, dived, caught fire,
turned over, and, carried along by the west wind,
fell on its back at Beuvraigne. The passenger fell
out at Bus, the pilot at Tilloloy. . . ."

When the victor landed at Beuvraigne near his
victim, the artillerymen belonging to a nearby
battery of 95 mm. guns (47th battery of the 31st
regiment of artillery), and who were already crowd-
ing around the enemy's body, rushed upon and
surrounded Guynemer. But the commander, Captain Allain Launay, mustered his men, ordered a
salute to Guynemer, made a speech to his command, and said: "We shall now fire a volley in
honor of Sergeant Guynemer." The salvo demolished a small house where some Boches had taken
refuge. Through the binoculars they could be seen
to scatter when the first shell struck their shelter.

"They owe that to me, too!" cried the enthusiastic urchin.

Meanwhile Captain Allain Launay had patiently
ripped the captain's stripes from his cap, and
when he had finished handed them to Guynemer:

"Promise me to wear them when you are appointed captain."

This victory was not questioned, and there was even some discussion about making this youngster a Knight of the Legion of Honor. But even when he had been promoted sergeant there had been some objection, owing to his youth. "Nevertheless," Guynemer had observed angrily, "I am not too young to be hit by the enemy's shells." This time another objection arose: If he receives the "cross" for this victory, what can be given him for succeeding ones? The proud little Roland rebelled, revolted, rose up like a cock on its spurs. He did not see that everybody already foresaw his destiny. He would have his "cross," he would have it, and he would not wait long for it, either. He would know how to wring it out of them.

Six days later, December 14, with his comrade, the sober and calm Bucquet, he attacked two Fokkers, one of which was dashed to pieces in its fall, while the other damaged his own machine. A letter to his father described the combat in his own brief and direct manner, without a superfluous word: "Combat with two Fokkers. The first, trapped, and his passenger killed, dived upon me without having seen me. Result: 35 bullets at close quarters and '*couic*' [his finish]! The fall was seen by four other airplanes (3 plus 1 makes 4, and perhaps that will win me the 'cross'). Then combat with the second Fokker, a one-seated machine shooting through the propeller, as rapid and easily handled as mine. We fought at ten meters, both turning vertically to try to get behind.

"My spring was slack: compelled to shoot with one hand above my head, I was handicapped; I was able to shoot twenty-one times in ten seconds. Once we almost telescoped, and I jumped over him — his head must have passed within fifty centimeters of my wheels. That disgusted him; he went away and let me go. I came back with an intake pipe burst, one rocker torn away: the splinters had made a number of holes in my overcoat and two notches in the propeller. There were three more in one wheel, in the body-frame (injuring a cable), and in the rudder."

All these accounts of the chase, cruel and clear, seem to breathe a savage joy and the pride of triumph. The sight of a burning airplane, of an enemy sinking down, intoxicated him. Even the remains of his enemies were dear to him, like treasures won by his young strength. The shoulder-straps and decorations worn by his adversary who fell at Tilloloy were given over to him; and Achilles before the trophies of Hector was not more arrogant. These combats in the sky, more than nine thousand feet above the earth, in which the two antagonists are isolated in a duel to the death, scarcely to be seen from the land, alone in empty space, in which every second lost, every shot lost, may cause defeat — and what a defeat! falling, burning, into the abyss beneath — in which they fight sometimes so near together, with short,

unsteady thrusts, that they see each other like
knights in the lists, while the machines graze and
clash together like shields, so that fragments of
them fall down like the feathers of birds of prey
fighting beak to beak — these combats which require the simultaneous handling of the controlling
elements and of the machine-gun, and in which
speed is a weapon, why should they not change
these young men, these children, into demi-gods?
Hercules, Achilles, Roland, the Cid — where shall
we find outside of mythology or the epics any
prototypes for the wild and furious Guynemer?

On the day of his coming of age, December 24,
1915 — earlier than his ancestor under the Empire
— he received the Cross of the Legion of Honor,
with this mention: "Pilot of great value, model of
devotion and courage. Has fulfilled in the past
six months two special missions requiring the
finest spirit of sacrifice, and has waged thirteen
aërial combats, two of which ended in the enemy
airplanes falling in flames." This mention was already behindhand, having been based upon the
report dated December 8. To the two victories
therein mentioned should be added those of the
5th and the 14th of December. Decorated at the
age of twenty-one, the enlisted mechanician of
Pau continued to progress at breakneck speed.
The red ribbon, the yellow ribbon and green War
Medal with four palms, are very becoming to a
young man's black coat. Georges Guynemer never
despised these baubles, nor in any way concealed
the pleasure they afforded him. He knew how high

one has to climb to pick them. And he was eager for more and more, not because of vanity, but for what they signified.

On the 3d and 5th of February, 1916, new combats took place, always in the region of Roy and Chaulnes. On February 3 he met three enemies within forty minutes, on the same round: "Attacked at 11.10 an L. V. G., which replied with its machine-gun. Fired 47 shots at 100 meters; the enemy airplane dived swiftly down to its own lines, smoking. Lost to view at 500 meters from the ground. At 11.40 attacked an L. V. G. (with Parabellum) from behind, at 20 meters; it tacked and dived spirally, pursued neck to neck at 1300 meters. It fell three kilometers from its lines. I rose again and lost sight of it. (This airplane had wings of the usual yellow color, its body was blue like the N., and its outlines seemed similar to that of the *monococques*.) At 11.50 attacked an L. V. G., which immediately dived into the clouds and disappeared. Landed at Amiens." He cleared the sky of every Boche: one fallen and two put to flight is not a bad record. He always attacked. With his accurate eyes he tracked out the enemy in the mystery of space, and placing himself higher, tried to surprise him. On the 5th, near Frise, he closed the road to another L. V. G. which was returning to its lines, attacked it from above in front, tacked over it, reached its rear, and overwhelmed it like a thunder-clap. The Boche fell in flames between Assevillers and Herbécourt. One more victory, and this one had the honor of

appearing in the official *communiqué*. Sometimes
he got back with his machine and his clothes
riddled with bullet-holes. He carried fire and
massacre up into the sky. And all this was nothing
as yet but the exercise of a knight-errant in his
infancy. This became evident later when he had
acquired complete mastery of his work.

February, 1916 — the month in which began the
longest, the most stubborn and cruel, and perhaps
the most significant battle of the Great War. In
this month began Verdun, and the menacing
German advance on the right of the Meuse (February 21-26), to the wood of Haumont, the wood
of the Caures and Herbebois, then to Samogneux,
the wood of the Fosses, the Le Chaume wood and
Ornes, and finally, on February 25, the attack on
Louvemont and Douaumont. The escadrilles, little
by little, headed in the same direction, and Guynemer was about to leave the Sixth Army. He would
dart no more above the paternal mansion, announcing his victories by his caracoles in the air;
nor watch over his own household during his
patrol of the region beyond Compiègne, over
Noyon, Chauny, Coucy, and Tracy-le-Val. The
cord which still linked him with his infancy and
youth was now to be strained, and on March 11
the Storks Escadrille received orders to depart
next day, and to fly to the Verdun region.

The development of the German fighting airplanes had constantly progressed during 1915.
Now, early in 1916, they appeared at Verdun,
more homogeneous and better trained, and in

possession of a series of new machines: small, one-seated biplanes (Albatros, Halberstadt, new Fokker, and Ago), with a fixed motor of 165–175 H.P. (Mercédès, and more rarely Benz and Argus), and two stationary machine-guns firing through the propeller. These chasing escadrilles (*Jagdstaffeln*) are essentially fighting units. Each *Jagdstaffel* comprises eighteen airplanes, and sometimes twenty-two, four of which are reserves. These airplanes do not generally travel alone, at least when they have to leave their lines, but fly in groups (*Ketten*) of five each, one of them serving as guide (*Kettenfuhrer*), and conducted by the most experienced pilot, regardless of rank. German aviation tactics seek more and more to avoid solitary combat and replace it by squadron fighting, or to surprise an isolated enemy by a squadron, like an attack of sparrow-hawks upon an eagle.

Ever since the establishment of our first autonomous group of fighting airplanes, which figured in the Artois offensives in May, 1915, but which did not take the offensive (having their cantonments in the barriers and limiting themselves to keeping off the enemy and cruising above our lines and often behind them), our fighting airplanes gradually overcame prejudice. They were not, it is true, so promptly brought to perfection as our army corps airplanes, which proved so useful in the Champagne campaign of September, 1915; but it was admitted that the aërial combat should not be regarded as a result of mere chance, but as inevitable, and that it constituted, first, a protection, and afterwards an effective obstruction to an enemy forbidden to make raids in our aërial domain. The next German offensive — against Verdun — had been foreseen. In consequence, the staff had organized a safety service to avoid all surprise by the enemy, to meet attacks, and prepare the way for the reinforcing troops. But the violence of the Verdun offensive exceeded all expectations.

Our escadrilles had done their duty as scouts before the attack. After it began, they were overwhelmed and numerically unable to perform all the aërial missions required. The fighting enemy escadrilles, with their new series of machines and their improvements, won for a few days the complete mastery of the air. Our own airplanes were forced off the battle-field, and driven from their landing-places by cannon. Meanwhile the Verdun battle was changing its character. General Pétain, who took command on February 26, restored the order which had been compromised by the bending of the front, and established the new front against which the Germans hurled their forces. It was also necessary for him to reconquer the mastery of the air. He asked for and obtained a rapid concentration of all the available escadrilles, and demanded of them vigorous offensive tactics. To economize and coördinate strength, all the fighting escadrilles at Verdun were grouped under the sole command of Major de Rose. They operated by patrols, sometimes following very distant itineraries, and attacking all the airplanes they met. In a short time we regained our air supremacy, and our airplanes which were engaged in regulating artillery fire and in taking aërial photographs could work in safety. Their protection was assured by raids even into the German lines.

The Storks Escadrille, then, flew in the direction of Verdun. In the course of the voyage, Guynemer brought down his eighth airplane, which fell vertically in flames. This was a good augury. Hardly had he arrived on March 15 when he began to explore the battle-field with his conqueror's eyes. The enemy at that time still thought himself master, and dared to venture within the French lines. Guynemer chased, over Revigny, a group of five airplanes, drove another out of Argonne, and while returning met two others, almost face to face. He engaged 'the first one, tacking under it and firing from a distance of ten meters. But the adversary answered his fire, and Guynemer's machine was hit: the right-hand rear longitudinal spar was cut, the cable injured, the right forward strut also cut, and the wind-shield shattered. The airman himself was wounded in the face by fragments of aluminum and iron, one lodging in the jaw, from which it could never be extracted, one in the right cheek, one in the left eyelid, miraculously leaving the eye unhurt, while smaller fragments peppered him generally, causing hemorrhages which clogged his mask and made it adhere to the flesh. In addition, he had two bullets in his left arm. Though blinded by blood, he did not lose his sang-froid, and hastily dived, while the second airplane continued firing, and a third,

furnished with a turret, which had come to the
rescue of its comrades, descended after him and
fired down upon his machine. Nevertheless, he had
escaped by his maneuver, and in spite of his
injuries made a good landing at Brocourt. On the
14th he was evacuated to Paris, to the Japanese
ambulance in the Hotel Astoria, and with despair
in his soul was obliged to let his comrades fight
their battle of Verdun without his help.

III. "LA TERRE A VU JADIS ERRER DES PALADINS...."[1]

At Verdun our aërial as well as our land forces
underwent sudden and almost prodigious reverses.
Within a few days the Storks Escadrille had been
decimated: its chief, Captain Brocard, had been
wounded in the face by a bullet and compelled
to land; Lieutenant Perretti had been killed,
Lieutenant Deullin wounded, Guynemer wounded
and nearly all its best pilots put *hors de combat*.
The lost air-mastery was only regained by the
tenacity of Major de Rose, Chief of Aviation of
the Second Army, and by a rapid reconcentration
of forces.

Major de Rose ordered enemy-chasing, and
electrified and inspired his escadrilles. The part he
played during those terrible Verdun months can
never be sufficiently praised. Guynemer's comrades held the sky under fire, as their brothers,
the infantrymen, held the shifting ground which

[1] "Once knightly heroes wandered over earth...."

protected the ancient citadel. Chaput brought down seven airplanes, Nungesser six, and a drachen, Navarre four, Lenoir four, Auger and Pelletier d'Oisy three, Puple, Chainat, and Lesort two. The observation airplanes rivaled the fighting machines, often defending themselves, and not infrequently forcing down their assailants in flames. Twice Sergeant Fedoroff rid himself in this manner of troublesome adversaries. But other pilots deserve to be mentioned, pilots such as Stribick and Houtt, Captain Vuillemin, Lieutenant de Laage, Sergeants de Ridder, Viallet and Buisse, and such observers as Lieutenant Liebmann, who was killed, and Mutel, Naudeau, Campion, Moulines, Dumas, Robbe, Travers, *sous-lieutenant* Boillot, Captain Verdurand — admirable squadron chief — and Major Roisin, expert in bombardments. The lists of names are always too short, but these, at least, should be loudly acclaimed.

Meanwhile the battle of Verdun shattered trees, knocked down walls, annihilated villages, hollowed out the earth, dug up the plains, distorted the hills, and renewed once more that chaos of the third day, according to Genesis, on which the Creator separated the waters from the earth. Almost the entire French army filed through this extraordinary epic battle, and Guynemer, wounded and weeping with rage, was not there.

But there was another period in the Great War in which the grouping of our fighting escadrilles and their employment in offensive movements gave us triumphant superiority in the aërial struggle, and this was the battle of the Somme, particularly during its first three months — a splendid and heroic time when our airmen sprang up in the sky, spreading panic and fear, like the knights-errant of *La Légende des siècles*. Victor Hugo's verses seem to describe them and their vertiginous rounds rather than the too slow horsemen of old:

La terre a vu jadis errer des paladins;
Ils flamboyaient ainsi que des éclairs soudains,
Puis s'évanouissaient, laissant sur les visages
La crainte, et la lueur de leurs brusques passages . . .
Les noms de quelques-uns jusqu'à nous sont venus. . . .
Ils surgissaient du Sud ou du Septentrion,
Portant sur leur écu l'hydre ou l'alérion,
Couverts des noirs oiseaux du taillis héraldique,
Marchant seuls au sentier que le devoir indique,
Ajoutant au bruit sourd de leur pas solennel
La vague obscurité d'un voyage éternel,
Ayant franchi les flots, les monts, les bois horribles,
Ils venaient de si loin qu'ils en étaient terribles,
Et ces grands chevaliers mêlaient à leurs blasons
Toute l'immensité des sombres horizons. . . .

These new knights-errant who wandered above the desolate plains of the Somme, no longer on earth but in the sky, mounted on wingèd steeds, who started up with a "heavy sound" from south or north, will be immortal like those of the ancient epics. It will be said that it was Dorme or Heurtaux, or Nungesser, Deullin, Sauvage, Tarascon, Chainat, or it was Guynemer, who accomplished such and such an exploit. The Germans, without knowing their names, recognized them, not by their armor and their sword-thrust, but by their machines, their maneuvers and methods. Almost invariably their enemies desperately avoided a fight with them, retreating far within their own lines, where, even then, they were not sure of safety. Those who accepted their gage of battle seldom returned. The enemy aviation camps from Ham to Péronne watched anxiously for the return of their champions who dared to fight over the French lines. None of them cared to fly alone, and even in groups they appeared timid. In patrols of four, five, and six, sometimes more, they flew beyond their own lines with the utmost caution, fearful at the least alarm, and anxiously examining the wide and empty sky where these mysterious knights mounted guard and might at any moment let loose a storm. But in the course of these prodigious first three months of the battle of the Somme, our French chasing-patrols not infrequently flew to and fro for two hours over German aviation camps, forcing down all those who attempted to rise, and succeeding in spreading terror and consternation in the enemy's lines.

The Franco-British offensive began on July 1, 1916, on the flat lands lying along both banks of the Somme River. The general plan of these operations had been agreed upon in the preceding December. The battle of Verdun had not prevented its execution which, on the contrary, was expected to relieve Verdun. The attack was made on a front of 40 kilometers between Gommécourt

on the north and Vermandovillers on the south
of the river. From the beginning the French penetrated the enemy's first lines, the 20th Corps took
the village of Curlu and held the Favière wood,
while the 1st Colonial Corps and one division of
the 35th Corps passed the Fay ravine and took
possession of Bacquincourt, Dompierre and Bussus.
On the third, this successful advance continued
into the second lines. Within just a few days
General Fayolle's army had taken 10,000 prisoners, 75 cannon, and several hundred machine-guns.
But the Germans, who were concentrated in the
Péronne region, with strong positions like Maurepas, Combles, and Cléry, and, further in the rear,
Bouchavesnes and Sailly-Saillisel on the right
bank, and Estrées, Belloy-en-Santerre, Barleux,
Albaincourt and Pressoire on the left bank, made
such desperate resistance that the struggle was
prolonged into mid-winter. The German retreat in
March, 1917, to the famous Hindenburg line was
the strategic result of this terrible battle, the
tactics of which were continuously successful and
the connection between the different arms brought
to perfection, while the infantry made an unsur-
passed record for suffering and endurance and will
power in such combats as Maurepas (August 12),
Cléry (September 3), Bouchavesnes (September
12) — where, when evening came, the enemy was
definitely broken — and the taking of Berny-en-
Santerre, of Deniécourt, of Vermandovillers (September 13) on the left bank, and on the right bank
the entry into Combles (surrounded on September

26), the advance on Sailly-Saillisel and the stubborn defense of this ruined village whose château and central district had already been occupied on October 15, and in which a few houses resisted until November 12. Then, there was the fight for the Chaulnes wood, and La Maisonnette and Ablaincourt and Pressoire; and everywhere it was the same as at Verdun: the woods were razed to the ground, villages disappeared into the soil, and the earth was so plowed and crushed and martyred that it was nothing but one immense wound.

Now, the air forces had had their part in the victory. Obliged, as they were at Verdun, to resist the numerical superiority of the enemy, they had thrown off the tyranny of atmospheric conditions and accepted and fulfilled diverse missions in all kinds of weather. Verdun had hardened them, as it had "burned the blood" of the infantry who had never known a worse hell than that one. But as our operations now took the initiative, the aviation corps was able to prepare its material more effectively, to organize its aërodromes and concentrate its forces beforehand. Its advantage was evident from the first day of the Somme offensive, not only in mechanical power, but in a method which coördinated and increased its efforts under a single command. Though this arm of the service was in continuous evolution, more subject than any other to the modifications of the war, and the most susceptible of all to progress and improvement, it had nevertheless finished its trial stages and acquired full development as connecting agent

for all the other arms, whom it supplied with
information. Serving at first for strategic reconnaissance, and then almost exclusively for regulating artillery fire, the aërial forces now performed
complex and efficient service for every branch of
the army. By means of aërial photography they
furnished exact knowledge of the ground and of
the enemy's defenses, thus preceding the execution
of military operations. They regulated artillery
fire, followed the program laid down for the
destruction of the enemy, and supplied such
information as was necessary to set the time for
the attack. They then accompanied the infantry
in the attack, observed its progress, located the
conquered positions, revealed the situation of the
enemy's new lines, betrayed his defensive works,
and announced his reinforcements and his counter-
attacks. They were the conducting wire between
the command, the artillery, and the troops, and
everybody felt them to be sure and faithful allies,
for they were able to see and know, to speak and
warn. But the air forces, during all their useful
missions, were themselves in need of protection,
and there must be no enemy airplanes about if
they were to make their observations in security.
But how to rid them of these enemies, and render
the latter incapable of harm? Here the air cavalry,
the airplanes built for distant scouting and combats, intervened. The safety of observation machines could only be insured by long-distance
protection, that is to say, by aërial patrols taking
the offensive, not by a solitary guard, too often

disappointing, and ineffective against a resolute
adversary. Their safety near to the army could
be guaranteed only by carrying the aërial struggle
over into the enemy's lines and preventing all
raids upon our own. The groups belonging to our
fighting escadrilles on both banks of the Somme
achieved this result.

The one-seated Nieuport, rapid, easily managed,
with high ascensional speed, and capable, by its
solid construction and air-piercing power, of diving
from a height upon an enemy and falling upon
him like a bird of prey, was then the chasing airplane *par excellence*, and remained so until the
appearance of the terrible Spad, which made its
début in the course of the Somme campaign,
Guynemer and Corporal Sauvage piloting the
first two of these machines in early September,
1916. They were armed with machine-guns, firing
forward, and invariably connected with the direction of the machine's motion. The Spad is an
extraordinary instrument of attack, but its defense lies only in its capacity for rapid displace-
ment and the swiftness of its evolutions. Its rear
is badly exposed: its field of visibility is very
limited at the sides, and objects can be seen only
above and below, — below, minus the dead angle
of the motor and the cock-pit. The pilot can easily
lose sight of the airplanes in his own group or that
of the enemy, so that if he is alone, he is in danger
of being surprised. On the other hand, one condition of his own victory is to surprise the enemy,
especially if he attacks a two-seated machine

whose range of fire is much broader, or if he does not hesitate to choose his victim from among a group. The Spad pilot makes use of the sun, of fog, of clouds. He flies high in order to hold the advantage of being able to pounce down upon his enemy while the enemy approaches prudently, timidly, suspecting no danger.

The battle of the Somme was the most favorable for solitary airplanes, or airplanes coupled like hunting-dogs. Since then methods have changed, and the future belongs to fighting escadrilles or groups of machines. But at that time the one-seated airplane was king of the air. One of them was enough to intimidate enemy airplanes engaged in regulating artillery fire and in short-distance scouting, making them hesitate to leave their lines, and to frighten barrier patrols of two or even four two-seated airplanes, in spite of their shooting superiority, into turning back and disbanding. The one-seated enemy machines never ventured out except in groups, and even with the advantage of two against one refused to fight. So the one-seated French machine was obliged to fly alone, for if it was accompanied by patrols, the enemy fled and there was no one to attack; whereas, when free to maneuver at will, the solitary pilot could plan ruses, hide himself in the light or in the clouds, take advantage of the enemy's blind sides, and carry out sudden destructive attacks which are impossible for groups. Our airmen never speak of the Somme without a smile of satisfaction: they have retained heroic memories of that campaign. Afterwards, the Germans drilled their one-seated or two-seated patrols, trained them in resistance to isolated attacks, and taught them in turn how to attack the solitary machine which had ventured out beyond its own lines. We were obliged to alter our tactics and adopt group formation. But the strongest types of our enemy-chasing pilots were revealed or developed during the battle of the Somme.

Moreover, our aviators at that time were incomparable; and in citing the most illustrious among them one risks injustice to their co-panions whose opportunities were less fortunate and whose exploits were less brilliant but not less useful. The cavalry, artillery, and infantry were drawn upon for recruits for the aviation branch of the army, and it appeared a difficult undertaking to fuse such different elements; but as all shared the same life and the same dangers, had similar tastes, and a passion for attaining the same result, and as their officers were necessarily recruited from among themselves, and chosen for services rendered, an atmosphere of *camaraderie* and friendly rivalry was created. A great novelist said that the origin of our friendships dates "from those hours at the beginning of life when we dream of the future in company with some comrade with the same ideals as our own, a chosen brother."[1] What difference does it make, then, if they depart in company for glory or for death? These young men gave themselves with the same willingness to the

[1] Paul Bourget, *Une Idylle tragique.*

same service, a service full of constant danger.
They were not gathered together by chance, but
by their vocation and by selection, and they spoke
the same language. For them, friendship easily became rivalry in courage and energy, and a school
of mutual esteem, in which each strove to outdo
the other. Friendship kept them alert, drove away
inertia and weakness, and they became confident
and generous, so that each rejoiced in the success
of the others. In the mountains, on the sea, in every
place where men feel most acutely their own
fragility, such friendship is not rare; but war
brings it to perfection.

The patrols of the Storks Escadrille, in the beginning of the Somme campaign, consisted of a
single airplane, or airplanes in couples. Guynemer,
whom everybody called "the kid," always took
Heurtaux with him when he carried a passenger;
for Heurtaux, as blond as Guynemer was brown,
thin and slender, very delicate and young, seemed
to give Guynemer the rights of an elder. Heurtaux
was the Oliver of this Roland. In character and
energy they were the same. Dorme used to take
Deullin with him, or de la Tour. Or the choice
was made alternately. This was the quartet of
whom the enemy had cause to beware, and woe
to the Boche who met any one of them! There was
at that time at Bapaume a group of five one-seated
German machines which never maneuvered singly.
If they perceived a pair of Nieuports, they immediately tacked about and fled in haste. But if one
of our chasers was cruising alone, the whole group

attacked him. Heurtaux, attacked in this way, had been compelled to dive and land, and on his return had to submit to the jests of Guynemer, for at that age friendship is roughish. "Go there yourself," advised Heurtaux, "and you will see." Next day Guynemer went alone, but in his turn was forced down. After these two trials, which might have ended in disaster — but knights must amuse themselves — the five one-seated planes at Bapaume were methodically but promptly beaten down.

Friendship demands equality between souls. If one has to protect the other, if one is manifestly superior, it is no longer friendship. In the Storks Escadrille friendship reigned in peace in the midst of war, so surely did each take his turn in surpassing the others. Which one was, finally, to be the greatest, not because of the number of his mentions, nor his renown or public fame, but according to the testimony of his comrades — the surest and most clearsighted of testimony — for no one can deceive his peers? Would it be the cold and calm Dorme, who went to battle as a fisher goes to his nets, who never spoke of his exploits, and whose heart, under this modest, gentle, kind exterior, was filled with hatred for the invader who occupied his own countryside, Briey, and for six months had held in custody and ill-treated his parents? In the Somme battle alone his official victories numbered seventeen, but the enemy could recount many others, doubtless, for this silent, well-balanced young man possessed quite improbable audacity. He would fly more than fifteen or twenty kilometers above the German lines, perfectly tranquil under the showers of shells which rose from the earth. At such a distance within their lines the Boche airplanes thought themselves safe when, suddenly, *du Sud ou du Septentrion,* appeared this knightly hero. And he would return smilingly, as fresh as when he had started out. It was only with difficulty that a very brief statement could then be extracted from him. His machine would be inspected, and not a trace of any fragment found; he might have been a tourist returning from a promenade. In more than a hundred combats his airplane received only three very small wounds. His cleverness in handling his machine was incredible: his close veering, his twistings and turnings, made it impossible for the adversary to shoot. He also knew how to quit the combat in time, if his own maneuvers had not succeeded. He seemed invulnerable. But later, much later, while he was fighting on the Aisne in May, 1917, Dorme, who had penetrated far within the enemy's lines, never came back.

Was Heurtaux the greatest, whose method was as delicate as himself — a virtuoso of the air, clever, supple and quick-witted, whose hand and eye equaled his thought in rapidity? Was it Deullin, skilled in approach, and prompt as the tempest? Or the long-enduring, robust, admirable *sous-lieutenant* Nungessor, or Sergeant Sauvage, or Adjutant Tarascon? Was it Captain Ménard, or Sangloer, or de la Tour? But the reader knows very well

IN THE AIR

that it was Guynemer. Why was it Guynemer, according to the testimony of all his rivals? History and the epic have coupled many names of friends, like Achilles and Patroclus, Orestes and Pylades, Nisus and Euryalus, Roland and Oliver. In these friendships, one is always surpassed by the other, but not in intelligence, nor courage nor nobility of character. For generosity, or wisdom of council, one might even prefer a Patroclus to an Achilles, an Oliver to a Roland. In what, then, lies the superiority? That is the secret of temperament, the secret of genius, the interior flame which burns the brightest, and whose appearances cause astonishment and almost terror, as if some mystery were divulged.

It is certain that Georges Guynemer was a mechanician and a gunsmith. He knew his machine and his machine-gun, and how to make them do their utmost. But there were others who knew the same. Dorme and Heurtaux were perhaps more skillful in maneuvering than he. (It was interesting to watch Guynemer when he was preparing to mount his Nieuport. First the bird was brought out of the shed; then he minutely examined and fingered it. This tall thin young man, with his amber-colored skin, his long oval face and thin nose, his mouth with its corners falling slightly, a very slight moustache, and crow-black hair tossed backward, would have resembled a Moorish chief had he been more impassive. But his features constantly showed his changing thoughts, and this play of expression gave grace and freshness to his face. Sometimes it seemed strained and hardened, and a vertical wrinkle appeared on his forehead above the nose. His eyes — the unforgettable eyes of Guynemer — round like agates, black and burning with a brilliance impossible to endure, for which there is only one expression sufficiently strong, that of Saint-Simon concerning some personage of the court of Louis XIV: "The glances of his eyes were like blows" — pierced the sky like arrows, when his practiced ear had heard the harsh hum of an enemy motor. In advance he condemned the audacious adversary to death, seeming from a distance to draw him into the abyss, like a sorcerer.)

After examining his machine he put on his fur-lined *combinaison* over his black coat, and his head-covering, the *passe-montagne*, fitting tightly over his hair, and framing the oval of his face, and over this his leather helmet. Plutarch spoke of the terrible expression of Alexander when he went to battle. Guynemer's face, when he rose for a flight, was appalling.

What did he do in the air? His flight journals and statements tell the story. On each page, a hundred times in succession, and several times on a page, his flight notebooks contain the short sentences which seem to bound from the paper, like a dog showing its teeth: "I attack ... I attack ... I attack...." At long intervals, as if ashamed, appears the phrase: "I am attacked." On the Somme more than twenty victories were credited to him, and to these should be added, as in the case of Dorme, others taking place at too great distances to receive confirmation. In the first month of the Somme battle, on September 13, 1916, the Storks Escadrille, Captain Brocard, was mentioned before the army: "Has shown unequaled energy and devotion to duty in the operations of Verdun and the Somme, waging, from March 19 to August 19, 1916, 338 combats, bringing down 36 airplanes, 3 drachen, and compelling 36 other badly damaged airplanes to land." Captain Brocard dedicated this mention to Lieutenant Guynemer, writing under it: "To Lieutenant Guynemer, my oldest pilot, and most brilliant Stork. Souvenir of gratitude and warmest friendship." And all the pilots of the escadrille, in turn, came to sign it. His comrades had often seen what he did in the air.

When Guynemer came back and landed, what a spectacle! Although a victor, his face was not appeased. It was never to be appeased. He never was satisfied, never waged enough battles, never burned or destroyed enough enemies. When he landed he was still under the influence of nervous effort, and seemed as if electrified by the fluid still passing through his frame. However, his machine bore traces of the struggle: four bullets in the wing, the body, and the elevator. And he himself was grazed by the missiles, his *combinaison* scratched and the end of his glove torn. By what miracle had he escaped? — He had passed through encircling death as a man leaps through a hoop.

His method was one of the wildest temerity and

impetuosity, and can be recommended to nobody. The number and strength of the enemy, so far from repelling, attracted him. He flew to vertiginous heights, and taking his place in the sunshine, watched and waited. In an attack he did not make use of the aërial acrobatic maneuvers with which, however, he was perfectly familiar. He struck without delay, — what is known in fencing as the cut direct. Without trying to maintain his machine within his adversary's dead angles, he fell on him as a stone falls. He shot as near to the enemy as he could, at the risk of being shot first himself, and even of interlocking their machines, though in that respect the sureness of his maneuvering sufficed to disengage him. If he failed to take the enemy by surprise, he did not quit the combat as prudence exacted; but returned to the charge, refusing to unhook his clutch from the enemy airplane, and held him, and wanted him, and got him.

His passion for flying never diminished. On rainy days, when it was unreasonable and useless to attempt to fly, he wandered around the sheds where the winged horses took their repose. He could not resist it: he entered, and mounted his own machine, settling himself in his cock-pit and handling the controls, holding mysterious conferences with his faithful steed.

In the air, he had a higher power of resistance than the most robust men. This frail, sickly Guynemer, twice refused by the army because of feebleness of constitution, never gave up. In proportion as the requirements of aviation became more severe, as the higher altitudes reached made it more exhausting, Guynemer seemed to prolong his flights to the point where overwork and nervous depression compelled him to go away and take a little rest — which made him suffer still more. And suddenly, before he had taken the necessary repose, he threw it off like ballast, and returning to camp, reappeared in the air, like the falcon in the legend of Saint Julien the Hospitaller: "The bold bird rose straight in the air like an arrow, and there could be seen two spots of unequal size which turned and joined, and then disappeared in the heights of heaven. The falcon soon descended, tearing some bird to pieces, and returned to his perch on the gauntlet, with his wings quivering."[1] Thus the victorious Guynemer came back, quivering, to the aviation field. Truly, a god possessed him.

Apart from all that, he was just a boy, simple, gay, tender, and charming.

IV. ON THE SOMME (JUNE, 1916, TO FEBRUARY, 1917)

Georges Guynemer, then, was wounded on March 15, 1916, at Verdun. On April 26, he arrived again at the front, with his arm half-cured and the wounds scarcely healed. He had escaped from the doctors and nurses. Between times, he had

[1] Flaubert.

been promoted *sous-lieutenant*. But he had to be sent back, to his bandages and massage.

He returned to Compiègne. The bargain he had made with his sister Yvonne was continued, and when the weather was clear he went to Vauciennes, where his machine awaited him. The first time he met an airplane after his fall and his wound, he experienced a quite natural but very painful sensation. Would he hesitate? Was he no longer the stubborn Guynemer? The Boche shot, but he did not reply. The Boche used up all his machine-gun belt, and the combat was broken off. Was it to be believed? What had happened?

Guynemer returned to his home. In the spring dawn comes very soon, and he had left so early that it was still morning. Was his sister awake? He waited, but waiting was not his forte. So he opened the door again, and his childish face appeared in the strip of light that filtered through. This time the sleeper saw him.

"Already back? Go back to bed. It is too early."

"Is it really so early?"

Her sisterly tenderness divined that he had something to tell her, something important, and that it would be necessary to help him to tell it. "Come in," she said.

He opened the blinds and sat down at the foot of the bed.

"What scouting have you done this morning?"

But he was following his own thoughts: "The men had warned me that under those circumstances one receives a very disagreeable impression."

"Under what circumstances?"

"When one goes up again after having been wounded, and meets a Boche. As long as you have not been wounded you think nothing can happen to you. When I saw that Boche this morning I felt something quite new. Then . . ."

He stopped and laughed, as if he had played some schoolboy joke.

"Then, what did you do?"

"Well, I made up my mind to submit to his shots. Calmly."

"Without replying?"

"Surely: I ordered myself not to shoot. That is the way one masters one's nerves, little sister. Mine are entirely mastered: I am now absolutely in control. The Boche presented me with five hundred shots while I maneuvered. They were necessary. I am perfectly satisfied."

She looked at him, sitting at the foot of the bed with his head resting against the post. Her eyes were wet and she kept silent. The silence continued.

Finally she said softly, "You have done well, Georges."

But he was asleep.

Later, referring to this meeting in which he offered himself to the enemy's fire, he said gravely:

"That was the decisive moment of my life. If I had not set things right then and there, I was done for. . . ."

When he reappeared at his escadrille's headquarters on May 18, quite cheerful but with a set
face and flaming eyes, no one dared discuss his
cure with him.

The Storks returned for a few days to the Oise
region, and once more the contented pilot of a
Nieuport flew over the country from Péronne to
Roye. He had not lost the least particle of his determination; quite the reverse. One day (May 22)
he searched the air desperately for three hours,
and though he finally discovered a two-seated
enemy machine over Noyon, he was obliged to
give over the combat for lack of gasoline in his
motor.

Meanwhile they were preparing the Somme
battle; the escadrilles familiarized themselves
with their ground, and new machines were tried.
The enemy, who suspected our preparations, sent
out long-distance scouting airplanes. Near Amiens,
above Villers-Bretonneux, Guynemer, making his
rounds with Sergeant Chainat, attacked one of
these groups on June 22, isolated one of the airplanes and, maneuvering with his comrade, set it
afire. That was, I believe, his ninth. This combat
took place at a height of 4200 meters. The advantage went more and more to the pilot who
mounted highest.

After July 1 there was a combat almost every
day. Would Guynemer be put out of action from
the beginning, as at Verdun? Returning on the
6th, after having put to flight an L. V. G., he
surprised another Boche airplane which was diving

down on one of our artillery-regulating machines. He immediately drew the enemy's attention to himself; but the enemy (Guynemer pays him this homage in his flight notebook) was keen and supple. His well-aimed shots passed through the propeller of the Nieuport and cut two cables in the right cell. Guynemer was obliged to land. He was forced down eight times during his flying career, once under fantastic conditions. He passed through every form of danger without ever losing the self-possession, the quickness of eye, and rapidity of decision which his passion for conquest had developed.

What battles he fought in the air! On July 9 his journal notes a combat of five against five; on the 10th a combat of three against seven, in which Guynemer disengaged Deullin, who was followed by an Aviatik at a distance of a hundred meters. On the 11th, at 10 o'clock, he attacked an L. V. G. and cut its cable; the enemy dived but appeared to be in control of the machine. A few moments later he and Deullin attacked an Aviatik and an L. V. G., Guynemer damaging the Aviatik, and Deullin forcing down the L. V. G.; and before returning to their base, the two comrades attacked a group of seven machines and dispersed them. On the 16th Guynemer forced down, with Heurtaux, an L. V. G., which fell with its wheels in the air. After a short absence, during which he got a more powerful machine for his own use, he began on the 25th a repetition of his former program. On the 26th he waged five combats with enemy

groups consisting of from five to eleven airplanes.
On the 27th he fought three L. V. G.'s, and then
groups of from three to ten machines. On the 28th
he successively attacked two airplanes within their
own lines, then a drachen which was obliged to
land, then a group of four airplanes one of which
was forced down, and then a second group of four
which were dispersed, Guynemer pursuing one of
the fugitives and bringing him down. One blade
of his own propeller was riddled with bullets, and
he was compelled to land. Such was his work for
three days, taken at random from the notebook.

Open his journal at any page, and it reads the
same. On August 7 Guynemer got back with seven
shell fragments in his machine: he had been cannonaded from the ground while in chase of four
enemy airplanes. On the same day he started off
again, piloting Heurtaux, who attacked the German trenches north of Cléry and fired on some
machine-guns. From its place up in the air the
airplane encouraged the infantry, and shared in
their assaults. The recital of events became, however, more and more brief: the fighting pilot had
not time enough to write details; nobody had any
time in the Storks Escadrille, constantly engaged
as it was in its triumphant flights. We must turn
then to Guynemer's letters — strange letters, indeed, which contain nothing, absolutely nothing
about the war, or the battle of the Somme, or
about anything else except *his* war and *his* battle.
The earth-world no longer existed for him: the
earth was a place which received the dead and the

vanquished. So this is the way in which he wrote his two sisters,. then sojourning in Switzerland (Fritz meaning any enemy airplane):

DEAR KIDS,

Some sport: the 17, attacked a Fritz, three shots and gun jammed; Fritz tumbled. The 18th, *idem*, but in two shots: two Fritzes in five shots, record.

Day before yesterday, attacked Fritz at 4.3o at ten meters: killed the passenger and perhaps the rest, prevented from seeing what happened by a fight at half-past four: the Boche ran.

At 7.4o attacked an Aviatik, carried away by the impetus, passed it at fifty centimeters; passenger "*couic*" (killed), the machine fell and was got under control again at fifty meters above the ground.

At 7.35, attacked an L. V. G.; at fifteen meters; just ready to shoot, when a bullet in. my fingers made me let go the trigger; reservoir burst, good landing two kilometers from the trenches between two shell-holes. Inventory of the "taxi": one bullet right in the face of my Vickers; one perforative bullet in the motor; the steel stone had gone clear through it as well as the oil reservoir, the gasoline tank, the cartridge chest, my glove ... where it stayed in the index finger: result, about as if my finger had been slightly pinched in a door; not even skinned, only the top of the nail slightly blackened. At the time I thought two fingers had been shot. To continue the inventory: one bullet in the reservoir, in the direction of my left lung, having passed through four millimeters of copper and had the good sense to stop, but one wonders why.

One bullet in the edge of the back of my seat, one in the rudder, and a dozen in the wings. They knocked the "taxi" to pieces with a hatchet at two o'clock in the

morning, under shell-fire. On landing, received 86 shots
of 105, 130 and 150, for nothing. They will pay the bill.

For a beginning, La Tour has his fourth mention.

A hug for each of you.

GEORGES.

P.S. — It could not be said now that I am not
strong; I stop steel bullets with the end of my finger.

Is this a letter? At first, it is a bulletin of victory:
two airplanes for five bullets, plus one passenger
"*couic.*" Then it becomes a recital of the golden
legend — the golden legend of aviation: he stops
the enemy's bullets with his fingers; Roland would
write in that style to the beautiful Aude: "Met
three Saracens, Durandal cleft two, the third tried
to settle 'the affair with his bow, but the arrow
broke on the cord." Young Paul Bailly was right:
"The exploits of Guynemer are not a legend, like
those of Roland; in telling them just as they happened we find them more beautiful than any we
could invent." That is why it is better to let
Guynemer himself relate them. He says only
what is necessary, but the right accent is there,
the rapidity and the "*couic.*" The following letter
is dated September 15, 1916.

From the same to the same

Some sport.

On the 16th, in a group of six, four of them squeezed
at 25 meters.

In four days, six combats at 25 meters: filled a few
Boches with holes, but they did not seem to tumble
down, though some were hard hit all the same; then

five boxing rounds up between 5100 and 5300 (altitude).
To-day five combats, four of them at less than 25
meters, and the fifth at 50 meters. In the first, gun
jammed at 50 meters. In the second, at 5200, the Boche
in his excitement lost his wings, and descended on his
aërodrome in a wingless coach; his ears must be
humming (16th). The third was a nose-to-nose combat
with a fighting Aviatik. Too much impetus: I failed to
hammer him hollow. In the fourth, same joke with an
L. V. G. in a group of three: I failed to hammer him,
I lurched: *pan*, a bullet near my head. In the fifth, I
cleaned up the passenger (that is the third this week),
then knocked up the pilot very badly at 10 meters, —
completely disabled, he landed evidently with great
difficulty, and he must be in hospital. . . .

Three lines to describe a victory, the sixteenth.
And what boarding of the adversary, from above
and from below! He springs upon the enemy, but
fails to go through him. Both speeds combined,
he does not make much less than 400 kilometers an
hour when he dives on him. The meeting and
shooting hardly last one second, after which the
combat continues, with other maneuvers. Some
savant should calculate the time allowed for sight
and thought in fighting such duels!

This was the period of the great series of combats on the Somme. The Storks Escadrille, which
was the first to arrive, waged battle uninterruptedly
for eight months. Other escadrilles came to the
rescue. Altogether they were divided into two
groups, one under the command of Major Féquant,
the other under that of Captain Brocard, ap-

pointed chief of battalion. It becomes impossible
to enumerate all Guynemer's victories, and we
can merely emphasize the days on which he surpassed himself. September 23 was a remarkable
day, on which he brought down two enemies and
had a fall from a height of 3000 meters. Little Paul
Bailly would hardly have believed that; he would
have said it was surely a legend, the golden legend
of aviation. Nevertheless, here is Guynemer's
statement, countersigned by the escadrille commandant:

"*Saturday, September* 23. — Two combats near
Eterpigny. At 11.20 forced down a Boche in flames
near Aches; at 11.21 forced a Boche to land,
damaged, near Carrépuy; at 11.25 forced down a
Boche in flames near Roye. At 11.30, was forced
down myself by a French shell, and smashed my
machine near Fescamps. . . ."

These combats occurred between Péronne and
Montdidier. To his father he wrote with more
precision, but in his usual elliptical style.

"*September* 22: Asphyxiated a Fokker in 30
seconds, tumbled down disabled.

"*September* 23: 11.20. — A Boche in flames
within our lines.

"11.21. — A Boche disabled, passenger killed.

"11.25. — A Boche in flames 400 meters from
the lines.

"11.25 and a half. — A 75 blew up my water
reservoir, and all the linen of the left upper plane,
hence a superb tail spin. Succeeded in changing
it into a glide. Fell to ground at speed of 160 or

180 kilometers: everything broken like matches, then the 'taxi' rebounded, turned around at 45 degrees, and came back, head down, planting itself in the ground 40 meters away like a post; they could not budge it. Nothing was left but the body, which was intact: the Spad is strong; with any other machine I should now be thinner than this sheet of paper. I fell 100 meters from the battery that had demolished me; they had not aimed at me, but they brought me down all the same, which they had no difficulty in recognizing; the shell struck me hard some time before exploding. The Boche fell close by Major Constantin's post. I picked up the pieces."

The group which he had attacked was composed of five airplanes, flying in *échelon*, three above, two below. The two which flew lowest were assaulted by one of our escadrilles, and the pilots, seeing a machine fall in flames, thought at first it was their own victory. "It was my first one, falling from the upper story," Guynemer explained drolly, in his Stanislas-student manner. With his "*terrible oiseau*" he had waged battle with the three pilots "of the upper story," and had forced them down one after the other. "The first one," he said, "had a half-burned card in his pocket which had certainly been given him that same morning, judging by the date, which read in German: 'I think you are very successful in aviation.' I have his photograph with his Gretchen. What German heads! He wore the same decorations as that one who fell in the Bus wood...." Is this not Achilles

setting his foot on Hector and taking possession
of his trophies? Guynemer's heart was stone to
his enemies. He saw in them the wrongs done to
France, the invasion of our country, the destruction of our towns and villages, our desolation, and
our dead, so many of our dead whose deserted
homes weep for them. His was not to give pity,
but to do justice. And in doing justice, when
an adversary whom he had forced down was
wounded, he brought him help with all his native
generosity.

For him, thirty seconds had separated the
Capitol from the Tarpeian Rock. After his triple
victory came his incredible fall, unheard of, fantastic, from a height of 3ooo meters, the Spad
falling at the highest speed down to earth, and
rebounding and planting itself in the ground like
a picket. "I was completely stupefied for twenty-
four hours, but have escaped with merely immense
fatigue (especially where I wear my looping-the-
loop straps, which saved my life), and a gash
in my knee presented to me by my magneto.
During that 3oo-meter tumble I was planning
the best way to hit the ground (I had the choice
of sauces): I found the way, but there were still
95 out of 100 chances for the wooden cross. *Enfin*,
all right!" And this postscript followed: "Sixth
time I have been brought down: record!"

Lieutenant V. F., of the Dragon Escadrille, col-
liding with a comrade's airplane at a height of
3ooo meters, had a similar fall onto the Avocourt
wood, and was similarly astounded to find himself

whole. He had continued maneuvering during the
five or six minutes of the descent. "Soon," he wrote,
"the trees of the Hesse forest came in sight; in
fact, they seemed to approach at a dizzy rate of
speed. I switched off so as not to catch fire, and
a few meters before reaching the trees I nosed up
my machine with all my strength so that it would
fall flat. There was a terrible shock! One tree
higher than the rest broke my right wings, and
made me turn as if I were on a pivot. I closed my
eyes. There was a second shock, less violent than
I could have hoped: the machine fell on its nose
like a stone, at the foot of the tree which had
stopped me. I unfastened my belt which, luckily,
had not broken, and let myself slip onto the
ground, amazed not to be suffering intense agony.
The only bad effects were that my head was heavy,
and blood was flowing through my mask. I breathed,
coughed, and shook my arms and legs, and was
dumbfounded to find that all my faculties func-
tioned normally...." Guynemer did not tell us so
much; but, as a mathematician, he calculated his
chances. He too had switched off, and with the
greatest sang-froid superintended, so to speak,
his fall. Its result was no less magical.

The infantrymen had observed this rainfall of
airplanes. The French plane reached the earth
just before its pilot's last victim fell also, in
flames. The soldiers pitied the poor victor, who
had not, as they thought, survived his conquest!
They rushed to his aid, expecting to pick him up
crushed to atoms. But Guynemer stood up without

aid. He seemed like a ghost; but he was standing, he was alive, and the excited soldiers took possession of him and carried him off in triumph. A division general approached, and immediately commanded a military salute for the victor, saying to Guynemer:

"You will review the troops with me."

Guynemer did not know how to review troops, and would have liked to go. He was suffering cruelly from his knee:

"I happen to be wounded, General."

"Wounded, you! It's impossible. When a man falls from the sky without being broken, he is a magician, no doubt of that. You cannot be wounded. However, lean upon me."

And holding him up, almost indeed carrying him, he walked with the young *sous-lieutenant* in front of the troops. From the neighboring trenches rose the sound of singing, first half-suppressed, and then swelling into a formidable roar: the *Marseillaise*. The song had sprung spontaneously to the men's lips.

Cerebral commotion required Guynemer to rest for a few days. But on October 5 he started off again. The month of October on the Somme was marked by an improvement in German aviation, their numbers being considerably reinforced and supplied with new tactics. Guynemer defied the new tactics of numbers, and in one day, October 17, attacked a group of three one-seated planes, and another group of five. A second time he made a sortie, and attacked a two-seated plane which was aided by five one-seated machines. On another occasion, November 9, he waged six battles with one-seated and two-seated machines, all of which made their escape, one after another, by diving. Still this was not enough, and he set forth again and attacked a group of one Albatros and four one-seated planes. "Hard fight," says the journal, "the enemy has the advantage." He broke off this combat, but only to engage in another with an Albatros which had surprised Lieutenant Deullin at 50 meters. On the following day, November 10, he added two more items to his list (making his nineteenth and twentieth): his first victim, at whom he had shot fifteen times from a distance less than ten meters, fell in flames south of Nesle; the other, a two-seated Albatros, 220 H. P. Mercédès, protected by three one-seated machines, fell and was crushed to pieces in the Morcourt ravine. This double stroke he repeated on the twenty-second of the same month (making his twenty-second and twenty-third), and again on January 23, 1917 (his twenty-sixth and twenty-seventh), and still again the next day, the twenty-fourth (his twenty-eighth and twenty-ninth victories). In addition, here is one of his letters with a statement of the results of three chasing days. There are no longer headings or endings to his letters; he makes a direct attack, as he does in the air.

26-1-'17

January 24, 1917. — Fell on a group of five Boches
at 2300. I brought them back, with drums beating, at
800 meters (one wire stay cut, one escape pot broken).
At the end of the boxing-round, 400 meters above
Roye, I succeeded in getting behind a one-seated machine of the group. My motor stopped; obliged to
pump and let the Boche go.

11.45. — Attacked a Fritz, let him go at 800 meters,
my motor spattered, but the Boche landed, head down,
near Goyancourt. I only count him as damaged.

At this instant, I see a Boche cannonaded at 2400,
hence at 11.50 a boxing round necessary with a little
Rumpler armed with two machine-guns. The pilot got
a bullet in his lung; the passenger, who fired at me, got
one in his knee. The two reservoirs were hit, and the
whole machine took fire and tumbled down at Lignières,
within our lines. I landed alongside; in starting in
again one wheel was broken in the plowed frozen earth.
In taking away the "taxi" the park people completely
demolished it for me. It was rushed to Paris for repairs.

25. — I watch the others fly, and fume.

26. — Bucquet loaned me his "taxi." No view-finder;
only a wretchedly bad (oh, how bad!) sight-line.

At 12 o'clock. — Saw a Boche at 3800; took the lift.
— Arrived at the sun. — In turning, was caught in an
eddy-wind, rotten tail spin. — While coming down
again I saw the Boche aiming at me 200 meters away;
sent him ten shots: gun jammed; but the Boche seemed
excited and dived with his motor in full blast straight
south. Off we go! But I took care not to get too near so
that he would not see that my gun was out of action.
The altimeter tumbled: 1600 Estrées-Saint-Denis came
in sight. I maneuvered my Boche as well as I could.

Suddenly he righted himself and departed in the direction of Rheims, banging away at me.

I tried bluffing; I rose 500 meters and let myself fall on him like a pebble. When I began to think my bluff had not succeeded, he seemed impressed and began to descend again. I placed myself at a distance of 10 meters, but every time I showed my nose the passenger aimed at me. The road to Compiègne: 1000 ... 800 meters. When I showed my nose, the passenger, standing, stopped aiming and made a sign that he gave himself up. All right! I saw under his belly that four shells had struck the mark. 400 meters: the Boche slowed up his "*moulin*" (motor). 200 meters, 20 meters. I let him go and watched him land. At 100 meters I circled and found I was over an aërodrome. But, having no more cartridges, I could not prevent them from setting fire to their "taxi," a magnificent 200 H. P. Albatros. When I saw they had been surrounded, I landed and showed the Boches my broken machine-gun. Sensation. They had fired at me two hundred times: my bullets, before the breakdown, had gone through their altimeter and their tachometer, which had caused their excitement. The pilot said that an airplane had been forced down two days before at Goyancourt: passenger killed, pilot wounded in legs — had to have one amputated above the knee. I hope this original confirmation will be accepted, which will make 30.

Thirty victories, twenty or twenty-one of which occurred on the Somme: such is the schedule of these extraordinary flights. The last one surpassed all the rest. He fought unarmed, with nothing but his machine, like a knight who, with sword broken, manages his horse and brings his adversary to bay. What a scene it was when the German pilot and passenger, prisoners, became aware that Guynemer's machine-gun had been out of action! Once more he had imposed his will upon others, and his power of domination had fascinated his enemies.

In the beginning of February, 1917, the Storks Escadrille left the Somme after six months' fighting, and flew into Lorraine.

CANTO III
AT THE ZENITH

I. ON THE 25TH OF MAY, 1917

THE destiny of a Guynemer is to surpass himself. Part of his power, however, must lie in the
perfection of his weapons. Why could he not forge
them himself? In him, the mechanician and the
gunsmith were impatient to serve the pilot and
the fighter. Nothing in the science of aviation was
unknown to him, and Guynemer in the factory
was always the same Guynemer. He worked with
the same nervous tension when he overhauled his
machine-guns to avoid the too frequent and too
troublesome jamming, or when he improved the
arrangement of the instruments and tools in his
airplane in accordance with his superior practical
experience, as when he chased an enemy. He
wanted to compel the obedience of matter, as he
compelled the enemy to surrender.

In the Somme campaign he had forced down two
airplanes in a single day, and then four in two
days. In Lorraine he was to do even better. At
that time, the beginning of 1917, the German
aërial forces were very active in Lorraine, but the
city of Nancy paid no attention to them. In 1914
Nancy had seen the invading army broken against

the mountain of Saint Genevieve and the Grand
Couronné; she had withstood a bombardment by
gigantic shells and visits from air squadrons, and
all without losing her good humor and her ani-
mation. She was one of those cities on the front
who are accustomed to danger, and who find in it
an inspiration for courage, for commerce, and even
for pleasure which does not belong to cities behind
the lines. Sometimes people who were dining on
the Place Stanislas left their tables to watch some
fine battle in the air, after which they resumed
their seats and their appetites, merely replacing
Rhenish by Moselle wines. Nevertheless, the
frequency of raids, and the destruction caused by
bombs, began to make the existence of both
native and visiting Nancyites decidedly unpleasant.
The Storks Escadrille, which arrived in February,
very promptly punished these aërial brigands, by
a police policy both rapid and severe. The enemy
airplanes which flew over Nancy were vigorously
chased, and less than a month later the framework
of a good dozen of them, arranged in an orderly
manner around the statue of Stanislas Leczinski,
reassured the population and served as an interesting spectacle for the visitor who could no longer
have the pleasure of admiring, behind Lamour's
gates, the two monumental fountains consecrated
to Neptune and Amphitrite, by Guibal, and which
were then covered by coarse sacks of earth.

Guynemer had contributed his share of these
spolia opima. On March 16 he alone had forced
down three Boches, and a fourth on the 17th.

Three victories in one day constituted a novel exploit. Navarre had achieved a double victory on February 26, 1916, at Verdun, and Guynemer had the same success on the Somme; in this campaign Nungesser had burned a drachen and two airplanes in one morning; but three airplanes destroyed in one day had never been seen before.

On that same evening Guynemer wrote to his family, and I transcribe the letter just as it is, with neither heading nor final formula. The King of Spain, in *Ruy Blas*, talks of the weather before he tells of the six wolves he has killed; but the new Cid fought in all weathers and speaks of nothing but his chase:

9 o'clock. — Rose from the ground on hearing shell explosions. Forced down in flames a two-seated Albatros at 9.08.

9.20. — Attacked with Deuillin a group of three one-seated Albatros, famous on the Lorraine front. At 9.26 I brought one down almost intact: pilot wounded, Lieutenant von Hausen, nephew of the general. And Deullin brought down another in flames at the same time. About 9 o'clock Dorme and Auger had attacked and grilled a two-seated plane. These four Boches were in a quadrilateral, the sides of which measured five kilometers, four and a half kilometers, three kilometers and three kilometers. Those who were in the middle need not have bothered themselves, but they were completely distracted.

14.30. — Forced down a two-seated Albatros in flames.

Three Boches within our lines for my day's work.
... Ouf! G. G.

Guynemer, who had been promoted lieutenant in February and was to be made captain in March, treated this Lieutenant von Hausen humanely and courteously as soon as he had landed. In all his mentions up to that time Guynemer had been described as a "brilliant chasing pilot"; he was now mentioned as an "incomparable chasing pilot."

Early in April the Storks left Lorraine and went to make their nests on a plateau on the left bank of the Aisne, back of Fismes. New events were in preparation. After the German retreat to the Hindenburg line, the French army in connection with the English army — which was to attack Vimy cliffs (April 9–10, 1917) — was about to undertake that vast offensive operation which, from Soissons to Auberive in Champagne, was to roll like an ocean wave over the slopes of the Chemin des Dames, the hills of Sapigneul and Brimont, and the Moronvillers mountain. Hearts were filled with hope, and the men were inspired by a sacred joy. Their sufferings and their wounds did not prevent the hearts of the soldiers in that spring of 1917 from flowering in sublime sacrifices for the cause of liberty.

As at the battle of the Somme, so at the battle of the Aisne our aërial escadrilles were in close touch with the general staff and the other arms of the service. Their success was no doubt dependent upon the quality of the airplanes, and the factory output, and limited by the enemy's power in the

air. But though they were unable to achieve the
mastery of the air from the very first, they continued obstinately to increase their force, and little
by little their successes increased. They had to
oppose an enemy who had just accomplished an
immense improvement in his aviation corps.

In September, 1916, the German staff, profiting
by the lessons of the Somme campaign during
which its aviation forces had been so terribly
scourged, resolved upon an almost complete re-
organization of its aëronautical service. Hindenburg's program arranged for a rehandling of both
the direction and the technical services. A decree
dating from November, 1916, announced the
separation from the other services of the Air Fight
Forces (*Luftstreitkräfte*), which were to be placed
under a staff officer, the *Kommandeur der Luftstreitkräfte*. This new *Kommandeur*, who was to super-
intend the building of the machines as well as the
training of the pilots, was Lieutenant General von
Hoeppner, with Lieutenant Colonel Tjomsen as
an assistant. The squadrons, numbering more than
270, were divided into bombing, chasing, patrolling
and field escadrilles, these last being intrusted
with scouting, photographing, and artillery work,
in constant touch with the infantry. Most of these
novelties were servilely copied from French aviation. The Germans had borrowed the details of
liaison service, as well as those for the regulation
of artillery fire, from the French regulations. The
commander of the aëronautical section of the
Fifth German Army (Verdun) said in a report

that "a conscientious aviator was the only reliable
informant in action." And his supreme chief, the
Kronprinz, commenting upon this sentence, drew
the following conclusions: "All this shows once
more that through methodical use of Infantry
Aviation, the command can be kept informed of
developments through the whole battle. But the
necessary condition for fruitful work in the field
lies in a previous training carried on with the
infantry, machine-guns, artillery, and *liaison* units.
The task of the Infantry Flyer is apt to become
more difficult as the weather grows worse, and
ground more deeply plowed up, the enemy more
pressing, or our own troops yielding ground. When
all these unfavorable circumstances are united,
the Infantry Aviator can only be effective if he has
perfect training. So he must be in constant contact with the other services, and the Infantry
must know him personally. At a pinch he ought
to make himself understood by the troops, even
without any of the usual signals."

But these airplanes, while doing this special
work, must be protected by patrolling escadrilles.
The best protection is afforded by the chasing
units, fitted to spread terror and death far afield,
or to stop enemy escadrilles bound on a similar
errand. Here again, copying the French services,
Germany strengthened her chasing escadrilles
during the whole winter of 1916–1917, and by
the following spring she possessed no less than
forty. Before the war she had given her attention
almost exclusively to heavy airplanes. French

types were plagiarized: as the Morane had been altered into the Fokker, the Nieuport became an Albatros. Their one-seated 160 H. P. Albatros, with a Benz or Mercédès fixed engine and two Maxim guns shooting through the propeller, was henceforth the typical chasing machine. However, the powerful two-engine Gothas (520 H. P.) and the Friedrichshafen and A. E. G. (450 H. P.) soon made their appearance in bombing escadrilles.

At the same time, the defensive attitude adopted at the beginning of the Somme campaign was repudiated. The order of the day became strong concentration, likely to secure, at least in one sector, decided superiority in the air, even if other sectors must be left destitute or battle shirked. The flying men were never to be over-worked, so as to be fresh in an emergency. The subordination of aviation to the other services was evidently an inspiration from the French regulation saying: "The aviation forces shall be always ready to attack, but in perfect subordi-nation to the orders of the commanding officers."

In spite of this *readiness to attack*, the enemy recommended prudence in scouting and patrolling work. The airman was not to engage in a fight without special orders. He seldom cruises by him-self, and most often is one of five. To one Boelcke, fond of high altitudes and given to pouncing falconlike on his prey, like Guynemer, there are scores of Richtofens who, under careful protection from other airplanes, circle round and round trying to attract the enemy, and unexpectedly

getting behind him by a spiral or a loop. It should
be said here that the German controlling boards
take the pilot's word concerning the number of
his victories instead of requiring, as the French do,
the evidence of eye witnesses. The high figures
generously allowed to a Richtofen or a Werner
Voss are less creditable than the strictly controlled
record of a Guynemer, a Nungesser, or a Dorme.

The enemy expected in April, 1917, a massive
attack from the French air forces in the Aisne,
and had taken measures to evade it. An order from
the staff of the Seventh Army says that all flying
units shall be given the alarm whenever a large
number of French airplanes are sighted. The German machines must return to camp at once, refusing combat except on equal terms; and balloons
must be lowered, or even pulled down to the
ground. If, on the contrary, the German machines
took the offensive, the order was that, at the hour
determined upon, all available machines must rise
together to a low altitude, and divide into two
distinct fleets, the chasing units flying above the
rest. These two fleets must then make for the
point of attack, gaining height as they go, and
must engage the enemy above the lines with the
utmost energy, never giving up the pursuit until
they reach the French lines, when the danger from
anti-aircraft batteries becomes too great.

From this it is evident that the preference of
German Aviation for taking the offensive was not
sufficient to induce it to offer battle above the
enemy lines, and the tendency of the staff was to

group squadrons into overpowering masses. The French had preceded their opponents in the way of technical progress, but the Germans made up for the inferiority, as usual, by method and system. The French were unrivaled for technical improvements, and the training of their pilots. Their new machine, the Spad, was a first-rate instrument, superior in strength, speed, and ease of control to the best Albatros, and the Germans knew that this inferiority must be obviated. All modern battles are thus preceded by technical rivalry. The preparation in factories, week after week, and month after month, ultimately results in living machinery which the staff uses as it pleases.

Living machinery it is, but it is in appearance only that it seems to be independent of man. A battle is a collective work, to which each participant, from the General-in-chief to the road-mender behind the lines, brings his contribution. Colossal though the whole seems, perfect as the enormous machine seems to be, it would not work if there were not behind it a weak man made of poor flesh. A humble gunner, the anonymous defenders of a trench, a pilot who purges the air of the hostile presence, an observer who secures information in good time, some poor soldier who has no idea that his individual action was connected with the great drama, has occasionally brought about wonderful results — as a stone falling into a pool makes its presence felt to the remotest banks.

Amidst the fighters on the Aisne, Guynemer

was at his post in the Storks Escadrille. "All right!
(sic) they tumble down," he wrote laconically to
his family. There were indeed some five tumbling
down: on May 25 he had surpassed all that had
been done so far in aërial fights, bringing down
four German machines in that one day. His notebook states the fact briefly:

8.3o. — Downed a two-seater, which lost a wing as
it fell and was smashed on the trees 1200 meters NNE.
of Corbeny.

8.31. — Another two-seater downed, in flames, above
Juvincourt. — With Captain Auger, forced another
two-seater to dive down to 600 meters, one kilometer
from our lines.

Downed a D. F. W.[1] in flames above Courlandon.

Downed a two-seater in flames between Guignicourt
and Condé-sur-Suippes. Dispersed with Captain Auger
a squadron of six one-seaters.

Now, his Excellency, Lieutenant General von
Hoeppner, *Kommandeur der Luftstreitkräfte*, being
interviewed two days later by newspaper men he
had summoned for the purpose, told them and
through them told Germany and, if possible, the
whole world, that the German airplanes and

[1] The D. F. W. (*Deutsche Fleugzeg Werke*) is a scouting
machine provided with two machine-guns, one shooting
through the propeller, the other mounted on a turret aft.
It is thirty-nine feet across the wings, and twenty-four in
length. One Benz six-cylinder engine of 200/225 H.P. Its
speed at an altitude of 3000 meters supposed to be 150 kilometers an hour. One of these machines has been on view
at the Invalides since July, 1917.

the German airmen were unrivaled. "As for the French aviators," he went on to say remarkably apropos, "they only engage our men when they are sure of victory. When they have doubts about their own superiority, they prefer to desist rather than take any risks." This solemn lie the newspaper men repeated at once in their issues of May 28.

A few months later one of these same reporters, reverting to the subject of French aviation, took Guynemer himself to task in the *Badische Presse* for August 8, 1917, as follows: "The airman you see flying so high is the famous Guynemer. He is the rival of the most daring German aviators, an *as*, as the French call their champions. He is undoubtedly to be reckoned with, for he handles his machine with absolute mastery, and he is an excellent shot. But he only accepts an air fight when every chance is on his side. He flies above the German lines at altitudes between 6000 and 7000 meters, quite out of range of our anti-aircraft artillery. He cannot make any observations, for from that height he sees nothing clearly, not even troops on the march. He is exclusively a chasing flyer bent on destroying our own machines. He has been often successful, though he cannot be compared to our own Richtofen. He is very prudent; always flying, as I said above, at an altitude of at least 6000 meters, he waits till an airplane rises from the German lines or appears on its way home. Then he pounces upon it as a falcon might, and opens fire with his machine-gun. When he only wounds the pilot, or if our airman seems to show fight, Guynemer flies back to his own lines at the incredible speed of 250 kilometers an hour, which his very powerful machine makes possible. He never accepts a fair fight. Every man chases as he can."

"Every man chases as he can." Quite so. To revert to that 25th of May, the "very prudent" Guynemer, on his morning patrol, met three German airplanes flying towards the French lines. They were two-seaters, less nimble, no doubt, than one-seaters, but provided with so much more dangerous arms. Naturally he could not think of attacking them, "not feeling sure of victory," and "always avoiding a risky contest!" Yet he pounced upon his three opponents, who promptly turned back. However, he overtook one, began making evolutions around him, succeeded in getting slightly below him, fired, and with his first volley succeeded in bringing him down in flames north of Corbeny (northeast of Craonne).

The danger for a one-seater is to be surprised from behind. Just as Guynemer veered round, he saw another machine flying after him. He again fired upwards, and the airplane fell in flames, like the first, only a few seconds having elapsed between the two fights. Guynemer then returned to camp.

But he was excited by these two fights; his nerves were strained and his will was tense. He soon started again. Towards noon a German machine appeared above the camp itself. How had it been able to get there? This is what the airmen down below were asking themselves. It was useless to chase it, for it would take any of them longer to rise than the German to escape. So they had to content themselves with looking up, some of them searching the sky with binoculars. Everybody was back except Guynemer, when somebody suddenly cried:

"Here comes Guynemer!"

"Then the Boche is done for."

Guynemer, in fact, was coming down upon his prey like lightning, and the instant he was behind and slightly beneath him, he fired. Only one shot from the machine-gun was heard, but the enemy airplane was already spinning down, its engine going full speed, and was dashed into the earth at Courlandon near Fismes. The pilot had been shot through the head.

In the afternoon the very prudent Guynemer started for the third time, and towards seven o'clock, above the Guignicourt market gardens (that is to say, in the enemy lines), he brought down another machine in flames.

"Very prudent" is the last epithet one could have expected to see in connection with the name of Guynemer. For he rarely came home without bullet-holes in his wings or even in his clothes. The Boche, being the Boche, had shown his usual respect for truth and generosity towards an adversary.

Guynemer, when returning to camp after a victory, generally announced his success by making his engine work to some tune. This time the cadence was the tune of the *Lampions*. All the neighboring airplane sheds understood, also the cantonments, parks, depots, dugouts, field hospitals and railway stations; in a word, all the communities scattered behind the lines of an army. This time the motor was singing so insistently that everybody, with faces upturned, concluded that their Guynemer had been "getting them."

In fact, the news was already spreading like wildfire, as news has the mysterious capacity for doing. No, it was not simply one airplane he had set ablaze; it was two, one above Corbeny, the other above Juvincourt. And people had hardly realized the wonderful fact before the third machine was seen falling in flames near Fismes. It was seen by hundreds of men who thought it was about to fall upon them, and ran for shelter. Meanwhile, Guynemer's engine was singing.

And for the fourth time it was heard again at twilight. Could it be possible? Had Guynemer really succeeded four times? Four machines brought down in one day by one pilot was what no infantry-man, gunner, pioneer, territorial, Anamite or Senegalese had ever seen. And from the stations, field hospitals, dugouts, depots, parks and cantonments, while the setting sun lingered in the sky on this May evening, whoever handled a shovel, a pickaxe or a rifle, whoever laid down rails, unloaded trucks, piled up cases, or broke stones on the road, whoever dressed wounds, gave medicine or carried dead men, whoever worked, rested, ate or drank — whoever was alive, in a word —

stepped out, ran, jostled along, arrived at the camp, got helterskelter over the fences, broke into the sheds, searched the airplanes, and called to the mechanicians in their wild desire to see Guynemer. There they were, a whole town of them, knocking at every door and peeping into every tent.

Somebody said: "Guynemer is asleep."

Whereupon, without a word of protest, without a sound, the crowd streamed out and scattered in the darkening fields, threading its way back to the quiet dells behind the lines.

So ended the day of the greatest aërial victory.

II. A VISIT TO GUYNEMER

Sunday, June 3, 1917. To-day, the first Sunday of June, the women from the neighboring villages came to visit the camp. Nobody is allowed to enter, but from the road you can see the machines start or land. The day was glorious, and the broad sun transfiguring these French landscapes, with their elongated valleys, their wooded ranges of hills, and generally harmonious lines suggested Greece, and one looked around for the colonnades of temples.

Beyond the rolling country rose the Aisne cliffs, where the fighting was incessant, though its roar was scarcely perceived.

Why had these villages been attracted to this particular camp? Because they knew that here, in default of Greek temples, were young gods. They wanted to see Guynemer.

The news had flown on rapid wings from hamlet to hamlet, from farm to farm, of what had happened on the 25th, and on the next day Guynemer had been almost equally successful.

Several aviators had already landed, men with famous names, but the public cannot be expected to remember them all. Finally an airplane descended in graceful spirals, landing softly and rolling along close to the railings.

"*Guynemer!*"

But the pilot, unconscious of the worshiping crowd, took off his helmet, disclosed a frowning face, and began discontentedly to examine his gun. Twice that day it had jammed, saving two Germans. Guynemer was like the painters of old who, by grinding their colors themselves, insured the duration of their works. He resented not being able to make all his weapons himself, his engine, his Vickers, and his bullets. At length he seemed willing to leave his machine, and pulled off his heavy war accouterment, which revealed a tall, flexible young man. As he rapidly approached his tent, his every motion watched by the onlookers, a private turned on him a small camera, with a beseeching —

"You'll permit me, *mon capitaine?*"

"Yes, but quick."

He was cross and impatient, and as he stopped he noticed all the eyes of the women watching him ecstatically. He made a despairing gesture. His frown deepened, his figure stiffened, and the snapshot was another failure.

Hardly any of his portraits are like him. Does
the fact that he was tall and spare, almost beard-
less, with an amber-colored, oval face and a regular profile, and raven-hair brushed backwards,
give any idea of the force that was in him? If his
eyes, dark with golden reflections, could have
been painted, they might no doubt have given a
more accurate notion of him: his capacity for sur-
veying all space, and his prompt decision, were
visible in them, as well as his carefulness and his
courage. Their glance was so direct, almost brutal,
that it could be felt, so to speak, physically; and
yet it could suddenly express a cheerful, boyish
nature, or disclose his close attention to the technical problems which everlastingly engrossed his
mind.

Guynemer was very different from Navarre,
with his powerful profile and broad chest like an
eagle in repose, and different from Nungesser, the
Nungesser before his wounds had so devastated
his body that a medical board wanted to declare
him unfit, a decision which he heroically resisted,
adding to his thirty victories another triumph
over physical disability. Guynemer differed from
them mentally, too, possessing neither their instinct nor their intuitiveness. These he replaced
with scientific accuracy based on study, by a
passion for flying, by method allied to fervor, by
violent logic. His power was nervous and almost
electric. The vicinity of danger drew sparks from
him.

His most daring exploits were prepared by medi-

tation beforehand, and he never indulged in recklessness without having pondered and calculated.
His action was so swift that it might seem in-
stinctive, but under appearances the reasoning
element was always present.

It was now late, but he was willing to talk to us
about that wonderful 25th of May, for he had no
objection to talking about his enemy-chasing;
on the contrary, he would tell us details with the
same amusement as if he related lucky plays at
poker, and with the same knowing ways. There was
not the least shade of affectation or of posing in
his narrative, but he talked with the simplicity
of a child. He told us that his third encounter had
been the most enjoyable. He was coming back to
lunch, had seen the impudent German soaring
above the camp, had fired, and the man had gone
down dead. After this exceedingly brief account
he laughed as usual, a fresh laugh like a girl's, and
his eyes closed. He said he was sleepy; he had been
out twice, and before he went again he wanted a
little rest.

I remember how bustling the camp looked! It
was half-past six, and the weather was wonderful,
with not a cloud in the sky, for some floating white
flakes in the blue could not be called clouds. But
these white flakes began to multiply; they were,
in fact, an enemy patrol, which had succeeded in
crossing the lines and was now above us. We
counted two, three, four machines, which the
sparks of our exploding shells promptly surrounded,

while three French Spads rose at full speed to meet them.

As we stood watching and wondering if the enemy would accept the fight, Guynemer suddenly appeared. He had been called, and now he and his comrades, Captain Auger and Lieutenant Raymond, came running to their machines. I watched Guynemer as he was being put into his leather suit. His whole soul was in his eyes, which glared at one moving point in space as if they themselves could shoot. Three of the German machines had already turned back, but the remaining one went on, insolently counting on his own power and speed. I shall never forget Guynemer, his face lifted, his eyes illuminated as if hypnotized by this point in space, his figure upright and stiffened like an arrow waiting to be released by the bow. Before pulling down his helmet he gave the order:

"Straight at him."

The engines snorted and snored, the propellers began to move, the machines rolled along, and suddenly were seen climbing almost vertically. Up above the fight was beginning, and it seemed as if the three starting airplanes could never reach in time the altitude of four or five thousand meters at which it was taking place.

The attacking Spad was obviously trying to get its opponent within firing range, but the German was a first-rate pilot and dodged without losing height, banking, looping, taking advantage of the Frenchman's dead angles, and striving to get him under his machine-gun. Round and round the two

airplanes circled, when suddenly the German
bolted in the direction of the Aisne cliffs. But the
Spad partly caught up with him and the aërial
circling began anew, while two other Spads appeared — a pack after a deer. The German
cleverly took advantage now of the sun, now of
the evening vapors, but he was within range, and
the tack-tack of a machine-gun was heard. Guynemer and the other two were coming nearer, when
the Spad dropped beneath its adversary and fired
upwards. The German plunged, and we expected
would sink, but he righted himself and was off in
an instant. However, this was Guynemer's chance:
three shots, not more, from his gun, and the German airplane crashed down somewhere near Muizon, on the banks of the Vesle.[1]

One after another, the victorious birds came
back to cover from every part of the violet and
rosy sky. But joy over their success must show itself, and they indulged in all the fanciful caprioles
of acrobatic aviation, spinning down in quick
spirals, turning somersaults, looping or plunging in
a glorious sky-dance. Last of these young gods,
Guynemer landed after one final circle, and took
off his helmet, offering to the setting sun his illuminated face, still full of the spirit of battle.

[1] This victory was not put down to Guynemer's account,
because another airman had shot first — which gives an
idea of the French controlling board's severity.

III. GUYNEMER IN CAMP

On the Somme Guynemer was one of the great
French champions; on the Aisne he became their
king. No enemy could resist him, and his daring
appeared without bounds. On May 27 he attacked
alone a squadron of six two-seaters above Auberive
at an altitude of 5000 meters, and compelled them
to go down to an altitude of 3600 meters. Before
landing, he pounced on another group of eight,
scattering them and bringing down one, completely
smashed, with its fuselage linen in rags, among
the shell-holes in a field. He was like the Cid
Campeador, to whom the Sheik Jabias said:

... Vous éclaties, avec des rayons jusqu'aux cieux,
Dans une préséance éblouissante aux yeux;
Vous marchiez, entouré d'un ordre de bataille;
Aucun sommet n'était trop haut pour votre taille,
Et vous étiez un fils d'une telle fierté
Que les aigles volaient tous de votre côté. ...

His feats exceeded all hopes, and his appearance
in the sky fairly frightened the enemy. On June 5,
after bringing down an Albatros east of Berry-au-
Bac, he chased to the east of Rheims a D. F. W.,
which had previously been attacked by other
Spads. "My nose was right on him," says Guynemer's notebook, "when my machine-gun jammed.
But just then the observer raised his hands. I
beckoned to him several times to veer towards our
lines, but noticing that he was making straight
for his own, I went back to my gun, which now

worked, and fired a volley of fifteen (at 2200 altitude). Immediately the machine upset, throwing the observer overboard, and sank on Berru forest." However, Guynemer's day's work was not done to his satisfaction after these two victories (his forty-fourth and forty-fifth): he attacked a group of three, and later on a group of four, and came back with bullets in his machine.

Meanwhile he had been made, on June 11, 1917, an Officer of the Legion of Honor with the following citation:

A remarkable officer, a daring and dexterous chaser. Has been of exceptional service to the country both by the number of his victories and by the daily example of his never-flagging courage and constantly increasing mastery. Careless of danger, he has become, by the infallibility of his methods, the most formidable opponent of German flyers. On May 25 achieved unparalleled success, bringing down two machines in one minute, and two more in the course of the same day. By these exploits has contributed to maintaining the courage and enthusiasm of the men who, from the trenches, have witnessed his triumphs. Forty-five machines brought down; twenty citations; twice wounded.

This document, eloquent and accurate and tracing facts to their causes, praises in Guynemer at the same time will-power, courage, and the contagion of example. Guynemer loved the last sentence, because it associated with his fights their daily witnesses, the infantrymen in the trenches.

The badge of an Officer in the Legion of Honor

was given to him at the aviation camp on July 5
by General Franchet d'Esperey, in command of
the Northern Armies. But this solemn ceremony
had not prevented Guynemer from flying twice,
the first time for two hours, the second flight one
hour, on a new machine from which he expected
wonders. He attacked three D. F. W.'s, and had
to land with five bullets in his engine and radiator.

His new decoration was given him at four o'clock
on a beautiful summer afternoon. Guynemer's
comrades were present, of course, and as pleased as
if the function had concerned themselves. The 11th
Company of the 82d Regiment of Infantry took
its station opposite the imposing row of squadron
machines, sixty in number, which stood there
like race horses as if to take part in the fête.
Guynemer's well-known airplane, the *Vieux-
Charles*, was the fifth to the left, its master having
required its presence, though it had been injured
that very day. In front of the aviation and regi-
mental flags the young aviator stood by himself in
his black *vareuse*, looking slight and pale, but
upright, with eyes sparkling. At a little distance
a few civilians — his own people, whom the general
had invited — watched the proceedings.

General Franchet d'Esperey appeared, a robust,
energetic man, and the following scene, described
by one of the trench papers — the *Brise d'enton-
noirs* of the 82d Infantry — took place: "The
general stopped before the young hero and eyed
him with evident pleasure; then he proclaimed him
a gallant soldier, touched his two shoulders with

his sword, as they did to champions of past ages, pinned the *rosette* on his coat, and embraced him. Then to the stirring tune of '*Sambre-et-Meuse*' the band and the soldiers marched in front of the new officer who, the ceremony now being over, joined his relatives some distance away."

General d'Esperey, looking over Guynemer's *Vieux-Charles*, noticed the damaged parts.

"How comes it that your foot was not injured?" he asked, pointing to one of the bullet-holes.

"I had just removed it, *mon général*," said Guynemer, with his usual simplicity.

None of the airmen with whom Guynemer shared his joy ever forgot that afternoon of July 5, 1917. The summer sun, the serene beauty of the hills bordering the Aisne, the distant bass of the battle, lent to the scene an enchanting but solemn interest. Tragic memories were in the minds of all the bystanders, and great names were on their lips — the names of retiring, noble, hard-working Dorme, reported missing on May 25, and of Captain Lecour-Grandmaison, creator of the three-seaters, who, on one of these machines, brought down five Germans, but was killed in a combat on May 10 and brought back to camp dead by a surviving comrade. Guynemer's red *rosette* meant glory to the great chasers, to wounded Heurtaux, to Ménard and Deullin, to Auger, Fonck, Jailler, Guérin, Baudouin, and all their comrades! And it meant glory to the pilots and observers who, always together in the discharge of duty, are not infrequently together in meeting death: to Lieu-

tenant Fressagues, pilot, and sous-lieutenant Bou-
vard, observer, who once fought seven Germans
and managed to bring one down; to Lieutenant
Floret and Lieutenant Homo, who, placed in
similar circumstances, set two machines on fire;
to Lieutenant Viguier who, on April 18, had the
pluck to come down to twenty-five meters above
the enemy's lines and calmly make his observations; and to so many others who did their duty
with the same daring, intelligence, and con-
scientiousness, to the hundreds of more humble
airmen who, while the infantry says the sanguinary
mass, throw down from above, like the chorister
boys in the *corpus Christi* procession, the red roses
of epics!

The whole Storks Escadrille had received from
General Duchêne the following *citation:* "Escadrille
No. 3. Commander: Captain Heurtaux. A brilliant
chasing escadrille which for the past two years has
fought in every sector of the front with wonderful
spirit and admirable self-sacrifice. The squadron
has just taken part in the Lorraine and Champagne operations, and during this period its members have destroyed fifty-three German machines
which, added to others previously brought down,
makes a total of one hundred and twenty-eight
certainly demolished, and one hundred and thirty-
two partly disabled."

This battle on the Aisne, with its famous climax
at the Chemin des Dames, began to slacken in
July; and it was decided that the chasing squadrons, including the Storks, should be transferred

to one of the British sectors where another offensive was being prepared. But before leaving the Fismes or Rheims district, Guynemer was active. He had not been given his new rank in the Legion of Honor to be idle: that was not his way. On the contrary, his habit was to show, after receiving a distinction as well as before, that he was worthy of it. On July 6 he engaged five two-seaters, and brought down one in flames. The next day his notebook records two more victories:

"Attacked with Adjutant Bozon-Verduraz, four Albatros one-seaters, above Brimont. Downed one in flames north of Villers-Franqueux, in our own lines. Attacked a D. F. W. which spun down in our lines at Moussy."

These victories, his forty-sixth, forty-seventh, and forty-eighth, were his farewell to the Aisne. But these excessive exertions brought on nervous fatigue. The escadrille had only just reached its new station, when Guynemer had to go into hospital, whence he wrote his father on July 18 as follows:

DEAR FATHER:

Knocked out again. Hospital. But this time I'm flourishing. No more wooden barracks, but a farmhouse right in the fields. I have a room all to myself. Quite correct: I downed three Fritzes, one ablaze, and the next day again great sport: mistook four Boches for Frenchmen. At first fought three of them, then one alone at 3200 to 800 meters. He took fire. They will have to wait till the earth dries so they can dig him out. An hour later a two-seater turned up at 5500. He blundered, and fell straight down on a 75, which died of the shock. But so did the passenger. The pilot was simply a bit excited, for which he couldn't be blamed. His machine had not plunged, but came down slowly, with its nose twirling, and I got his two guns intact. . . .

The *toubib* (doctor) says I shall be on my feet in three or four days. Don't see many Boches just now, but that won't last. I read in a newspaper that I had been mobbed in a friendly manner in Paris. I must be ubiquitous without knowing it. Modern science brings about marvels, modern journalism also.

Raymond has two strings (officer's stripes) and the cross of the Legion. Please congratulate him.

Good night, father.

GEORGES.

P.S. I, who get seasick over nothing at all, have just been out to sea for the first time. The water was very rough, especially for a little motor-boat, but I smiled serenely through it all. Wasn't I proud! . . .

In fact, some newspaper had announced that Guynemer would carry the aviation flag in the Parade of the Fourteenth of July in Paris, and this was enough to persuade the crowd that some other airman was Guynemer. Indeed, there had been talk of sending him to Paris on that solemn occasion, but he had declined. He loved glory, but hated show, and he had followed his squadron to Flanders, where he had taken to his bed.

The foregoing letter bears Guynemer's mark unmistakably. The son of rich parents rejoicing over having a room to himself, after having renounced all comfort from the very first day of his enlist-

ment, and willing to begin as *garçon d'aérodrome;*
the joke about the German airplane sunk so deep
in the wet ground that it would have to be dug
out, and the surprise of the pilot; the delight over
Raymond's promotion; the amusing allusion to
sea-sickness by the man who had no equal in air
navigation, are all characteristic details.

Sheik Jabias thus sums up his impressions after
visiting the Cid in his camp:

Vous dominiez tout, grand, sans chef, sans joug, sans
    digue,
Absolu, lance au poing, panache, au front. . . .

And that Cid had never fought up in the air.

IV. GUYNEMER IN HIS FATHER'S HOUSE

To quote him once more, Sheik Jabias, after being dazzled by the Cid in his camp, is supposed to
see him in his father's castle at Bivar, doing more
humble work.

. . . Que s'est-il donc passé? Quel est cet équipage?
J'arrive, et je vous trouve en veste, comme un page,
Dehors, bras nus, nu-tête, et si petit garçon
Que vous avez en main l'auge et le caveçon,
Et faisant ce qu'il sied aux écuyers de faire,
— Cheick, dit le Cid, je suis maintenant chez mon père.

Those who never saw Guynemer at his father's
at Compiègne cannot know him well. Of course,
even in camp he was the best of comrades, full of
his work, but always ready to enjoy somebody
else's success, and speaking about his own as if it

were billiards or bridge. His renown had not intoxicated him, and he would have been quite unconscious of it had he not sometimes felt that
unresponsiveness on the part of others which is
the price of glory: anything like jealousy hurt him
as if it had been his first discovery of evil. In
Kipling's *Jungle Book*, Mowgli, the man cub,
noticing that the Jungle hates him, feels his eyes
and is frightened at finding them wet. "What is
this, Bagheera?" he asks of his friend the panther.
"Oh, nothing; only tears," answers Bagheera, who
had lived among men.

One who, on occasion, told Guynemer *not to
mind* knows how deep was his sensitiveness, not to
the presence of real hostility, which he fortunately
never encountered, but even to an obscure germ of
jealousy. The moment he felt this he shrank into
himself. His native exuberance only displayed itself under the influence of sympathy.

Friendship among airmen is manly and almost
rough, not caring for formulas or appearances, but
proving itself by deeds. To these men the games of
war are astonishingly like school games, and are
spoken of as if they were nothing else. When a
comrade has not come back, and dinner has to begin without him, no show of sorrow is tolerated:
only these young men's hearts feel the absence of
a friend, and the casual visitor, not knowing, might
take them for sporting men, lively and jolly.

Guynemer was living his life in perfect confidence, feeling no personal ambition, not inclined
to enjoy honors more than work, ignoring all af-

fectation or attitudinizing, never politic, and
naturally unconscious of his own simplicity. Yet
he loved and adored what we call glory, and would
tell anybody of his successes, even of his decorations, with a childlike certitude that these things
must delight others as much as himself. His French
honors were of course his great pride, but he highly
appreciated those which he had received from
allied governments, too: the Distinguished Service
order, the Cross of St. George, the Cross of Leo-
pold, the Belgian war medal, Serbian and Mon-
tenegrin orders, etc. All these ribbons made a bright
show, and although he generally wore only the
rosette of the Legion of Honor, he would sometimes
deck himself out in them all, or carry them in his
pocket and occasionally empty them out on a
table, as at school he used to tumble out the untidy
contents of his desk in search of his task.

When he went to Paris to see to his machines, he
first secured a room at the Hôtel Edouard VII,
and immediately posted to the Buc works. When
he had time he would invite himself to dinner at
the house of his schoolmate at the Collège Stanislas, Lieutenant Constantin. "Every time he came,"
this officer writes, "some new exploit or a new
decoration had been added to his list. He never
wore all his medals, his 'village-band banner,' as
he amusingly called them; but when people asked
to see them, he immediately searched his pockets
and produced the whole disorderly lot. When he
became officer in the Legion, he appeared at my
mother's quite radiant, so that she asked him the

reason of this unusual joy. 'Regardez bien, madame, there is something new.' The new thing which my mother discovered was a tiny *rosette* ornamenting his red ribbon."

This *rosette* was so very small that nobody noticed it, and Guynemer felt that he must complain to the shopman at the Palais Royal who had sold it to him.

"Give me a larger one, a huge one," he said; "nobody sees this."

The tradesman spread a number of *rosettes* on his counter, but Guynemer only took back again the one of which he had complained, and went out laughing as if the whole thing had been a good joke.

His officer's stripes gave him as much pleasure as his decorations. Every time he was promoted, he wanted his stripes sewn on, not in a day or an hour, or even five minutes, but immediately. He received his captain's commission the same day he had been given the Distinguished Service order, and he promptly went to see his friend, Captain de la Tour, who was wounded in the hospital at Nancy. This officer had lost three brothers in action, and loved Guynemer as if he had been another younger brother. Indeed, Guynemer said later that La Tour loved him more than any other did.

"Don't you see any change in me?" Guynemer asked.

"No, you're just as usual."

"No, there's a change!"

"Oh, I see; you mean your English order; it does look well."

"There's something else. Look closer."

La Tour at last discovered the three stripes on the cap and sleeves.

"What! Are you a captain?"

"Yes, a captain," and Guynemer laughed his boyish laugh. — This kid a captain! So I am not an impressive captain, then? I haven't run risks enough to be a captain, probably! — His laugh said all this.

Lieutenant Constantin also says in his notes: "Guynemer disliked walking about Paris, because people recognized him. When he saw them turn to look at him, he would grumble at the curse of having a face that was public property. So he preferred waiting for evening, and then drove his little white car up the Champs Elysées to the Bois. He enjoyed this peaceful recreation thoroughly, and forgot the excitement of his life at the front. Memories of our boyhood days came back to him, and he dwelt on them with delight: 'Do you remember one day in *seconde* when we quarreled and fought like madmen? You made such a mark on my arm that it is there yet.' He did not mind, but I was ashamed of having been such a young brute. Another day, in May, 1917, coming home on leave I met Georges just as he stepped out of his hotel, and as I had just been mentioned in dispatches I told him about it. Immediately he dragged me into a shop, bought a *croix de guerre*, pinned it on my *vareuse*, and hugged me before everybody."

Guynemer had a genius for graciousness, and his imagination was inexhaustible when he wished to please, but his temper was hot and quick. One day he had left his motor at the door of the hotel, and some practical joker thought it clever to leave a note in the car with this inscription in large letters: AVIATORS TO THE FRONT! Guynemer did not take the joke at all, and was boiling with rage.

His complete freedom from conceit has often been remarked. At a luncheon given in his honor by the well-known deputy, Captain Lasies, he would not say a word about himself, but extolled his comrades until somebody said: "You are really modesty itself."

Whereupon another guest asked: "Could you imagine him bragging?"

Guynemer was delighted, and when the party broke up he went out with the gentleman who had said this and thanked him warmly. "Don't you see how little they understand? I don't say I am modest, but if I weren't I would be a fool, and I should not like to be that. I know quite well that just now some of us are getting so much admiration and so many honors that one may get more than one's share. Whereas the men in the trenches — how different it is with them!" [1]

But it was inevitable that he should be lionized. People came to him with albums and pictures.

[1] *Journal des Débats* for September 26, 1917.

He wrote to his father that a Madame de B. wanted something, just one sentence, in an album which was to be sold in America. "I am to be alongside the Generalissimo. What on earth can I write?"

An American lady who was also a guest at the Hôtel Edouard VII wanted to have at any price some souvenir of the young hero. She ordered her maid to bring away an old glove of Guynemer's which was lying on a chest of drawers, and replace it by a magnificent bouquet. "This lady put me in a nice dilemma," Guynemer explained, "as it was Sunday and there was no way of getting any more gloves." [1]

He had no affectation, least of all the kind that pretends to be ignorant of one's own popularity; but surely he cared little for popularity. Here again he puts us in mind of a medieval poem. In *Gilbert de Metz*, one of our oldest epics, the daughter of Anséis is described seated at the window, "fresh, slim, and white as a lily" when two knights, Garin and his cousin Gilbert, happen to ride near. "Look up, cousin Gilbert," says Garin, "look. By our lady, what a handsome dame!" "Oh," answers Gilbert, "what a handsome creature my steed is! I never saw anything so lovely as this maiden with her fair skin and dark eyes. I never knew any steed that could compare with mine." And so on, while Gilbert still refuses to look up at the beautiful daughter of Anséis. Also in *Girard de Viane*, Charlemagne, holding his

[1] Anecdote related in the *Figaro* for September 29, 1917.

COMBAT

court at the palace of Vienne, has just placed the hand of the lovely Aude in that of his nephew Roland. Both the girl and the great soldier are silent and blushing while the date of the wedding is being discussed, when a messenger suddenly rushes in: "The Saracens are in France! War! war!" shout the bystanders. Then without a word Roland drops the white hand of the girl, springs to arms, and is gone. So Guynemer would have praised his Nieuport or his Spad as Gilbert praised his steed, and *belle Aude* herself could not have kept him away from the fight.

One day his father felt doubts about the capacity of such a young man to resist the intoxication of so much flattery from men and women.

"Don't worry," Guynemer answered, "I am watching my nerves as an acrobat watches his muscles. I have chosen my own mission, and I must fulfil it."

After his death, one of his friends, the one who spoke to him last, told me: "He used to put aside heaps of flattering letters which he did not even read. 'Read them if you like,' he said to me, and I destroyed them. He only read letters from children, schoolboys and soldiers."

In *L'Aiglon* Prokesch brings the mail to the Prince Imperial, and handing him letters from women, he says:
Voilà
Ce que c'est d'avoir l'auréole fatale.

As soon as Prokesch begins to read them, the Prince stops him with the words: "*Je déchire.*"

Even when a woman whom he has nicknamed "Little Spring" — "because the water sleeping in her eyes or purling in her voice has often cooled his fever" — announces her departure, hoping he may detain her, he lets her go, whispering again like a refrain, "*Je déchire.*"

Did Guynemer deal with hearts as he dealt with the besieging letters, or as the falcon of St. Jean l'Hospitalier dealt with birds? — No "Little Spring," had her voice been ever so rill-like, could have detained him when a sunny morning invited him skywards.

Safe from the admiring public, Guynemer would relax and breathe freely with his people at Compiègne, where he became once more a lively, noisy, indulged, but coaxing and charming boy, except when absorbed in work, from which nothing could distract him. He spent hours in pasting and classifying the snapshots he took of his enemies just before pulling the trigger of his machine-gun and bringing them down. One of his greatest pleasures when on leave was to arrange and show these photographs.

His eyes, which saw everything, were keen to detect the least changes in the arrangement of his home, even when mere knickknacks had been moved about. At each visit he found the house ornamented with some new trophy of his exploits. He was delighted to find that a miniature barkentine, which he had built with corks, paper, and thread when he was seven years old, still stood on his mother's mantelpiece. Even at that age his powers of observation had been evident, and he had forgotten no detail of sails or rigging.

He had taken again so naturally his old place in the family circle that his mother forgot once and called the tall, famous young man by his old familiar name, "*Bébé*." She quickly corrected herself, but he said:

"I am always that to you, Mother."

"I was happier when you were little," she observed.

"I hope you are not vexed with me, Mother."

"Vexed for what?"

"For having grown up."

He was naturally full of the one subject that interested him, airplanes and chasing, and he would go round the house collecting audiences. Strange bits of narration could be overheard from different rooms as he held forth:

"Then I *embusqued* myself (became a slacker ..."

"What!"

"Oh! I *embusqued* myself behind a cloud."

Or, "The light dazzled me, so I hid the sun with my wing."

He never forgot his sisters' birthdays, but he could not always give them the present he preferred. "Sorry I could not present you with a Boche."

He was hardly different when his mother received company: he was never seen to play the

great man. Only on one subject he always and
instantly became serious, namely, when the future
was mentioned. "Do not let us make any plans,"
he would say.

A page from one of my own notebooks will help
to show Guynemer as I used to see him in his
home.

Wednesday, June 27, 1917. — Compiègne. Called on
the Guynemers. He is fascination itself with his "goddess
on the clouds" gait — as if he remembered when walking
that he could also fly — with his incomparable eyes, his
perpetual movement, his interior electricity, his admix-
ture of elegance and ardor, and with that impulse of his
whole being towards one object which suggests the
antique runner, even when he is for an instant in repose.
His parents and sisters do not miss a single gesture, a
single motion he makes. They drink in his every word,
and his life seems to absorb them. His laugh echoes in
their souls. They believe in him, are sure of him, sure
of his future, and that all will be well. Noticing this
certitude, whether real or assumed, I could not help
stealing a glance at the frail god of aviation, made like
the delicate statuettes that we dread breaking. He talks
passionately, as usual, of his aërial fights. But just now
one thought seems to supersede every other. He is
expecting a new machine, a magic machine which he
planned long ago, found difficult to get built, and with
which he must do more damage than ever.

Then he showed us his photographs with the white
blotches of bursting shells, or the gray wings of German
airplanes. One of these is seen as it falls in flames, the
pilot falling, too, some distance away from it.   Thus

the victim was registered, and the memory of it made
him happy.

I swallowed a question I was going to ask: What
about yourself — some day? because he looked so full
of life that the notion of death could never present
itself to him. But he seemed to have read my thoughts,
for he said:

"You have plenty of time in the air, except when you
fight, and then you have no time at all. I've been
brought down six times, and I always had plenty of
time to realize what was happening." And he laughed
his clear, boyish laugh.

As a matter of fact, he has been incredibly lucky.
In one fight he was hit three times, and each time the
bullet was deadened by some unexpected obstacle.

Finally I was shown photographs of himself, chrono-
logically arranged. Needless to say, it was not he who
showed them. There was the half-nude baby, with eyes
already sparkling and eager, then the school-boy with
the fine carriage of the head, then the lad fresh from
school with a singularly calm expression, and well filled-
out cheeks. A little later the expression appeared more
mature and tense, though still ingenuous. Later again
there was a decidedly stern look, with the face less oval
and thinner. The rough fingers of war had chiseled this
face, and sharpened and strengthened it. I looked from
the picture to him, and I realized that, compared to
his former pictures, his expression had now indeed
acquired something terrible. But just then he laughed,
and the laughter conjured away all phantasies.

V. THE MAGIC MACHINE

As a tiny boy who had invented an enchanted
bed for his sisters' dolls, as a boy who, at Collège
Stanislas, had rigged up a telephone to send messages to the last forms in the schoolroom, or manu-
factured miniature airplanes, as a recruit who, at
Pau, had gladly accepted the work of cleaning,
burnishing, and overhauling engines, Guynemer
had always shown a passion for mechanics. Becoming a pilot, and later on a chaser, he exhibited
in the study and perfecting of his airplanes the
same enthusiasm and perseverance as in his flights.
He was everlastingly calling for swifter or more
powerful machines, and not only strove to communicate his own fervor to technicians, but went
into minute details, suggested improvements, and
whenever he had a chance visited the workshops
and assisted at trials. Such trials are sometimes
dangerous. One of his friends, Edouard de Layens,
was killed in this kind of accident, and Guynemer
was enraged that a gallant airman should perish
otherwise than in battle. He was in reality an inventor, though this statement may cause surprise,
and though it may not be wise at present to
bear it out by facts.

Every part of his machine or of his gun was
familiar to him. He had handled them all, taking
them apart and putting them together again.
There are practical improvements in modern airplanes which would not be there had it not been
for him. And there is a "Guynemer visor."

Confidence and authoritativeness had not come
to him along with glory, for from the first he talked
as one engrossed by his ideas, and it is because he
was thus engrossed that he found persuasive words
to bring others round to his views. But, naturally
enough, he had not at first the prestige which he
possessed when he became Captain Guynemer,
had high rank in the Legion of Honor, and enjoyed world-wide fame. In his 'prentice days when,
in workshops or in the presence of well-known
builders, he would make confident statements,
inveigh against errors, or demand modifications,
people thought him flippant and saucy. Once
somebody called him a raw lad. The answer came
with crushing rapidity: "When you blunder, raw
lads like myself pay for your mistakes."

It must be admitted that, like most people
brought up with wealth, he was apt to be unduly
impatient. Delays or objections irritated him. He
wanted to force his will upon Time, which never
admits compulsion, and tried to over-ride obstacles.
His peculiar fascination gradually won its way
even in workshops, and his appearance there was
greeted with acclamation, not only because the
men were curious to see him, but because they
were in sympathy with him and had put his ideas
to a successful test. The workmen liked to see him
sit in a half-finished machine, and explain in his
short, decisive style what he wanted and what
was sure to give superiority to French aviation.
The men stopped work, came round, and listened
eagerly. This, too, was a triumph for him. What

he told them on such occasions he had probably
whispered to himself many times before when, on
rainy days, he would sit in his airplane under the
hangar, and think and talk to himself, while
strangers wondered if he was not crazy.

However, he had made friends with well-known
engineers, especially Major Garnier of Puteaux
and M. Béchereau of the Spad works. These two,
instead of dismissing him as a snappish airman
continually at variance with the builder, took his
inventions seriously and strove to meet his requirements. When M. Béchereau, after long delays, was at last decorated for his eminent services,
the Secretary of Aëronautics, M. Daniel Vincent,
came to the works and was going to place the
medal and red ribbon on the engineer's breast,
when he saw Guynemer standing near. He gra-
ciously handed the medal over to the airman,
saying:

"Give M Béchereau his decoration; it is only
fair you should."

In September, 1916, Guynemer had tried at the
front one of the first two Spads. On the 8th he
wrote to M. Béchereau: "Well, the Spad has had
her *baptême du feu*. The others were six: an Aviatik
at 2800, an L. V. G. at 2900, and four Rumplers
jostling one another with barely 25 meters in between at 3000 meters. When the four saw me coming (at 1800 on the speedometer) they no doubt
took me for a meteorite and funked, and when
they got over it and back to their shooting (fine
popping, though) it was too late. My gun never

jammed once." Here he went into technicalities about his new machine-gun, but further on reverted to the Spad: "She loops wonderfully. Her spin is a bit lazy and irregular, but deliciously soft." The letter concludes with many suggestions for minor improvements.

His correspondence with M. Béchereau was entirely devoted to a study of airplanes: he never wandered from the subject. Thus he collaborated with the engineer by constantly communicating to him the results of his experience. His machine-gun was the great difficulty. "Yesterday," he wrote on October 21, 1916, "five Boches, three of them above our lines, came within ten meters of the muzzle of my gun, and impossible to shoot. Four days ago I had to let two others get away. Sickening ... The weather is wonderful. Perhaps the gun will work now." In fact, a few days later he wrote exultingly, having discovered that the jamming was due to cold and having found an ingenious remedy.

November 4, 1916. Day before yesterday I bagged a Fokker one-seater biplane. It was two meters off, but as it tumbled into a group of our Nieuports, the controlling board would not give the victory to anybody. Yesterday got an Aviatik ten meters off; passenger shot dead by the first bullet; the plane, all in rags, went down in slow spirals and must have been knocked flat somewhere near Berlincourt. Heurtaux, who had seen it beginning to fall, brought one down himself ten minutes later, like a regular ball.

On November 18 next, after going into particulars concerning his engine which he wanted
made stronger, he told M. Béchereau of his 21st
and 22d victories:

As for the 21st, it was a one-seater I murdered as it
twirled in elegant spirals down to its own landing
ground. No. 22 was a 220 H.P., one of three above our
lines. I came upon it unawares in a somersault. Passenger stood up, but fell down again in his seat before
even setting his gun going. I put some two hundred or
two hundred and fifty bullets into him twenty meters
away from me. He had taken an invariable angle of 45°
on the first volley. When I let him go, Adjutant Bucquet
took him in hand — which would have helped if he
hadn't already been as full of holes as a strainer. He
kept his angle of 45° till about 500 meters, when he
adopted the vertical, and blazed up on crashing to the
ground. . . .

The Spad ravished him. It was the heyday of
wonderful flights on the Somme. Yet he wanted
something even better; but before pestering M.
Béchereau he began with an inspiring narrative.

December 28, 1916. I can't grumble; yet yesterday
I missed my camera badly. I had a high-class round with
an Albatros, a fine, clever fellow, between two and ten
meters away from me. We only exchanged fifteen shots,
and he snapped my right fore-cable — just a few threads
still held — while I shot him in the small of his back.
A fine spill! (No. 25).

Now, to speak of serious things, I must tell you that
the Spad 150 H.P. is not much ahead of the Halberstadt. The latter is not faster, I admit, but it climbs so

much more quickly that it amounts to the same thing. However, our latest model knocks them all out. . . .

The letter adds only some recommendations as to the necessity for more speed and a better propeller. But much more important improvements were already filling his mind. He had conceived plans for a magic airplane that would simply annihilate the enemy, and as he would doggedly carry on a fight, so he ruminated, begged, and urged until his idea was realized. But he was forced to practice exhausting perseverance, and on several occasions the lack of comprehension or sympathy which he encountered infuriated him. Yet he never gave up. It was not his way in a workshop, any more than in the air; and when, after some ten months' struggling, trying, and frequent beginning over again, he saw himself at last in possession of the wonderful machine, he rejoiced as a warrior may after forging his own weapons.

In January, 1917, he wrote to M. Béchereau urging him to make all dispatch: "Spring will soon be here, and the Germans are working like niggers. If we go to sleep, it will be '*couic*' for us." Henceforth his correspondence, sometimes rather dictatorial, with the engineer was entirely devoted to the magic airplane, — its size, controls, wing-tips, tank, weight, etc. The margins of his letters were covered with drawings, and every detail was minutely discussed. In February he wrote to his father as if he had been a builder: "My machine surpasses all expectations, and will soon be at work. In Paris I go to bed early and rise ditto, spending all day at Spad's. I have no other thought or occupation, It is a fixed idea, and if it goes on I shall become a perfect idiot. When peace is signed, let nobody dare to mention a weapon of any kind in my presence for six months."

He thought himself within reach of his goal; but unexpected obstacles would come in his way, and it was not till July 5, 1917 — the same day on which he received the *rosette* of the Legion of Honor from General Franchet d'Esperey at the Aisne Aviation Camp — that he could at last try the long-dreamed-of, long-hoped-for airplane. But in a fight against three D. F. W.'s, the splendid new machine got riddled with bullets, he had to land, and everything had to be begun over again. But Guynemer was not afraid of beginning over again, and in fact he was to give the airplane another chance in Flanders, and to see all his expectations fulfilled. The 49th, 50th, 51st and 52d victories of Guynemer were due to the magic airplane.

He managed to impose his will on matter, and on those who adapt it to the warlike conceptions of man, as he imposed it on the enemy. Then, spreading out his wings on high, he might well think himself invincible.

THE ASCENSION

I. THE BATTLE OF FLANDERS

AFTER the battle on the Aisne Georges Guynemer was ordered to Flanders, but he had to take
to his bed as soon as he arrived (July, 1917) and
only left the hospital on the 20th. He then repaired
to the new aviation camp outside Dunkirk, which
at that time consisted of a few rows of tents near
the seaside. He was to take part in the contem-
plated offensive, on his own magic airplane —
which he brought from Fismes on the 23d — for
the Storks Escadrille had been incorporated into a
fighting unit under Major Brocard. No disease
could be an obstacle to a Guynemer when an offensive was in preparation. In fact, all the Storks
were on the spot: Captain Heurtaux, now recovered from his wound received in Champagne
in April, was in command, and Captain Auger
(soon to be killed), Lieutenant Raymond, Lieutenant Deullin, Lieutenant Lagache and *sous-lieutenant* Bucquet were there; while Fonck and
Verduraz, newcomers to the squadron but not by
any means unknown, Adjutants Guillaumat, Henin,
and Petit-Dariel, Sergeants Gaillard and Moulines,

Corporals de Marcy, Dubonnet, and Risacher, completed the staff. As early as June 24 Guynemer had soared again.

In order to realize the importance of this new battle of Flanders which, begun on July 31, was to rage till the following winter, it may not be out of place to quote a German appreciation. In an issue of the *Lokal Anzeiger*, published at the end of September, 1917, after two months' uninterrupted fighting, Doctor Wegener wrote as follows:

How can anybody talk of anything but this battle of Flanders? Is it possible that some people actually grow hot over the parliamentarization, or the loan, or the cost of butter, or the rumors of peace, while every heart and every eye ought to be fixed on these places where soldiers are doing wonderful deeds! This battle is the most formidable that has yet been fought. It was supposed to be ended, but here it is, blazing afresh and promising a tremendous conflagration. The Englishman goes on with his usual doggedness, and the last bombardment has excelled in horrible intensity all that has been known so far. Even before the signal for storming, the English were drunk with victory, so gigantic was their artillery, so dreadful their guns, so intense their firing. . . .

These lines help us to realize how keen was the anxiety caused in Germany by the new offensive coming so soon after the battles of Champagne in April. But the lyricism of Dr. Wegener stood in the way of his own judgment, and prevented him from seeing that the battle on the Marne which drove the enemy back, the battle on the Yser which brought him to a standstill, and the battle round Verdun which effectually wore him out, were each in succession the greatest of the war. The second battle of Flanders ought rather to be compared to the battle on the Somme, the real consequences of which were not completely visible till the German recoil on the Siegfried line took place in March, 1917. While the first battle of Flanders had closed the gates of Dunkirk and Calais against the Germans, and marked the end of their invasion, the second one drove a wedge at Ypres into the German strength, made formidable by three years' daily efforts, secured the Flemish heights, pushed the enemy back into the bog land, and threatened Bruges. In the first battle, the French under Foch had been supported by the English under Marshal French; this time the English, who were the protagonists, under Plumer (Second Army) and Gough (Fifth Army), were supported by the First French Army under General Anthoine.

It was as late as June that General Anthoine's soldiers had taken their stand to the left of the British armies, and after the tremendous fights along the Chemin des Dames and Moronvillers in April, it might well be believed that they were tired. They had borne the burden from the very first; they had been on the Marne and the Yser in 1914, at the numberless and costly offensives of 1915 in Artois, Champagne, Lorraine and Alsace; and in 1916, after the Verdun epic, they had had to fight on the Somme. Indeed, they had only ceased repelling the enemy's attacks in order to attack in their turn. Among the Allies, they represented invincible determination, as well as a perfected military method. Those troops arriving on June 15, on ground they had never seen before, might well have been anxious for a respite; yet on July 31 they were in the fighting line with the British. Two days before the attack they crossed the Yser canal by twenty-nine bridges without losing one man, and showed an intelligence and spirit which added to their ascendancy over the enemy and increased the prestige of the French army. And while Marshal Haig was finding such an exceptional second in General Anthoine, Pétain, now commander-in-chief, was aiding the British offensive by attacking the Germans at other points on the front: on August 20 the Second Army under Guillaumat was victorious on the Meuse, near Verdun, while the Sixth Army under Maistre was preparing for the Malmaison offensive which on October 23 secured for the French the whole length of the Chemin des Dames to the river Ailette.

General Anthoine had had less than six weeks in which to see what he could do with the ground, organize the lines of communication, and post his batteries and infantry. But he had no idea of delaying the British offensive, and on the appointed day he was ready. The line of attack for the three armies was some 20 kilometers long, namely, from the Ypres-Menin road to the confluence of the Yperlée and Martje-Vaert, the French holding the section between Drie Grachten and Boesinghe. It

had been settled that the offensive should be conducted methodically, that its objective should be
limited, and that it might be interrupted and resumed as often as should seem advisable. The
troops were engaged on the 31st of July, and the
first rush carried the French onward a distance of
3 kilometers, not only to Steenstraete, which was
the objective, but further on to Bixchoote and the
Korteker Tavern. The British on their side had
advanced 1500 yards over heavily fortified or
wooded ground, and their new line lay along Pil-
kem, Saint-Julien, Frezenberg, Hooge, Sanctuary
Wood, Hollebeke and Basse-Ville. Stormy weather
on the first of August, and German counter-
attacks on Saint-Julien, prevented an immediate
continuation of the offensive, but on August 16 a
fresh advance took the French as far as Saint-
Jansbeck, while they seized the bridge-head of
Drie Grachten. General Anthoine had been so
careful in his artillery preparation that one of the
attacking battalions had not a single casualty,
and no soldier was even wounded. The French
then had to wait until the English had advanced
in their turn to the range of hillocks between
Becelaere and Poelcapelle (September 20 and 26),
but the brilliant British successes on those two
dates were making another collective operation
possible; and this operation took place on October
9, and gave the French possession of the outskirts
of Houthulst forest, while the British fought on
till they captured the Passchendaele hills.

Every great battle is now preceded and accompanied by a battle in the air, because if chasing or bombarding squadrons did not police the air before an attack, no photographs of the enemy's lines could be taken; and if they did not afford protection for the observers while the troops are engaged, the batteries would shoot and the infantry progress blindly. It is not surprising, therefore, that the enemy, who could not be deceived as to the importance of the French and British preparations in Flanders, had as early as mid-June brought additional airplanes and "sausages," and throughout July terrible contests took place in the air. Sometimes these engagements were duels, oftener they were fought by strong squadrons, and on July 13 units consisting of as many as thirty machines were seen on either side, the Germans losing fifteen airplanes, and sixteen more going home in a more or less damaged condition.

While in hospital, Guynemer had heard of these tremendous encounters, and wondered if the enchanting cruises he used to make by himself or with just one companion must be things of the past. Was he to be involved in the new tactics and to become a mere unit in a group, or a chief with the responsibility of collective maneuvers? The air knight was incredulous; he thought of his magic airplane and could not persuade himself that, whatever the number of his opponents, he could not single one out for his thunder-clap attack.

Meanwhile the artillery preparation had begun, towards the fifteenth of July, and the earth was quaking to the thundering front at a distance of 50 kilometers. These are flat regions, and there would be no beauty in them if the light radiating from the vapors rising from the fields or the sea did not lend brilliance and relief to the yellow stone villages, the straggling woods or copses, the well-to-do farms, the low hedges, or the tall calvaries at the crossroads.

Guynemer was in splendid condition. His indisposition of the previous month had been caused by his refusing to sleep at Dunkirk, as the others did, until their new quarters were ready. He wanted to be near his machine the moment there was light enough to see by, and slept in some unfinished hangar or under canvas in order not to miss any enterprising German who might take advantage of the dusk to sneak over the lines, spy on our preparations, or bombard our rear. He had paid for his imprudence by a severe cold. But now, comfortable-looking wooden houses stood along the shore, and Guynemer was himself again.

On July 27, while patrolling with Lieutenant Deullin, his chum of Somme and of Aisne days — in fact, his friend of much older times — he brought down in flames, between Langemark and Roulers, a very powerful Albatros, apparently a 220 H. P. of the latest model. This fell far within the enemy lines, but enthusiastic British soldiers witnessed the scene. Guynemer had chosen this Albatros for his victim among eight other machines, and had pulverized it at a distance of a few yards.

This victory was his forty-ninth. He secured his

fiftieth the very next day, bringing down a D. F. W. in flames over Westrobeke, the enemy showing fight, for Guynemer's magic airplane was hit in the tail, in one of the longitudinal spars, the exhaust pipe, and the hood, and had to be repaired. This day of glory was also one of mourning for the Storks. Captain Auger who, trusting his star after seven triumphs, had gone scouting alone, was shot in the head, and, after mustering energy enough to bring his machine back to the landing-ground, died almost immediately.

Fifty machines destroyed! This had been Guynemer's dream. The apparently inaccessible figure had gradually seemed a possibility. Finally it had become a fact. Fifty machines down, without taking into account those which fell too far from the official observers, or those which had been only disabled, or those which had brought home sometimes a pilot, sometimes a passenger, dead in their seats. What would Guynemer do now? Was he not tired of hunting, killing, or destroying in the high regions of the atmosphere? Did he not feel the exhaustion consequent on the nervous strain of unlimited effort? Could he be entirely deaf to voices which advised him to rest, now that he was a captain, an officer in the Legion of Honor, and, at barely twenty-two, could hardly hope for more distinction? On the other hand, he had shown in his unceasing effort towards an absolutely perfect machine a genius for mechanics which might profitably be given play elsewhere. The occasion was not far to seek, for he had to take his damaged

airplane back to the works; and what with this
interruption and the precarious state of his health
— for he had left the hospital too soon — he might
reasonably have applied for leave. Nor was this
all. The adoption of the new tactics of fighting in
numbers might change the nature of his action:
he might become the commanding officer of a unit,
run less risk, indulge his temerity only once in a
while, and yet make himself useful by infusing his
own spirit into aspiring pilots.

Slowly all these ideas occurred, if not to him, at
all events to his friends. Guynemer has slain his
fifty — they must have thought — Guynemer can
now rest. What would it matter if some envious
people should make remarks? "It is a pleasure
worthy of a king," Alexander once said after
Antisthenes, "to hear evil spoken of one while
one is doing good." But Guynemer never knew
this royal enjoyment; he never even suspected
that well-wishers were plotting for his safety. He
took his machine to the works, supervised the repairs with his customary attention, and by August
15 he was back again at his sport in Flanders.

Meanwhile his comrades had added to their
laurels. Auger was dead, it is true; but Captain
Derode, Adjutant Fonck — a perfect Aymerillot,
the smallest and youngest of these knights-errant,
Heurtaux, Deullin (both wounded, and the latter
now risen to a captaincy), Lieutenant Gorgeus
and Corporal Collins — all had done well. Besides
them many, too many, bombarding aviators ought

to be mentioned, but we must limit ourselves to those who are now laid low in Flemish graveyards: Lieutenant Mulard, Sergeant Thabaud-Deshoulières, *sous-lieutenant* Bailliotz, *sous-lieutenant* Pelletier, who saved his airplane if he could not save his own life, and was heard saying to himself before expiring: "For France — I am happy ...."; finally Lieutenant Ravarra, and Sergeant Delaunay, who had specialized in night attacks and disappeared without ever being heard of again.

Guynemer had reported at the camp on August 15. On the seventeenth, at 9.20 o'clock, he brought down a two-seated Albatros which fell in flames at Wladsloo, and five minutes later a D. F. W. which collapsed, also in flames, south of Dixmude. This double execution avenged the death of Captain Auger and of another Stork, Sergeant Cornet, killed the day before. On the eighteenth, Guynemer poured a broadside, at close quarters, into a two-seated machine above Staden; and on the twentieth, flying this time on his old *Vieux-Charles*, he destroyed a D. F. W. in a quick fight above Poperinghe. This meant three undoubted victories in four days under circumstances which the number of enemy machines and the high altitude made more difficult than they had ever been. The weather during this month of August was constantly stormy, and the Germans were taking every precaution to avoid surprise; but Guynemer was quick as lightning, took advantage of the shortest lulls, and baffled German prudence.

The British or Belgian airmen of the neighbor-
hood called on him, and he liked to return their
politeness. He loved to talk about his methods,
especially his shooting methods, for flying to him
was only the means of shooting, and once he de-
fined his airplane as a flying machine-gun. Captain
Galliot, a specialist in gunsmithery, who overheard this remark, also heard him say to the
Minister of Aviation, M. Daniel Vincent, who was
inspecting the camp at Buc: "It is not by clever
flying that you get rid of a Boche, but by hard
and sharp shooting."

It is not surprising, therefore, that he began his
day's work by overhauling his machine-gun,
cartridges, and visor. He did not mind trusting
his mechanicians where his airplane and motor
were concerned, but his weapon and ammunition
were his own special care. He regarded as an axiom
the well-known maxim of big-game hunters, that
"it is not enough to hit, but you must shoot down
your enemy with lightning rapidity if you do not
wish to perish with him. . . . " [1]

Of his machine itself Guynemer made a terrible
weapon, and he soon passed his fiftieth victory.
On August 20 his record numbered fifty-three,
and he was in as good condition as on the Somme.
On the 24th he was on his way to Paris, planning
not only to have his airplane repaired, but to point
out to the Buc engineers an improvement he had
just devised.

[1] *Guynemer tireur de combat* (*Guerre aérienne* for October
18, 1917, special number consecrated to Guynemer).

II. OMENS

"Oh, yes, the dog always manages to get what he wants," Guynemer's father had once said to him with a sad smile, when Georges, regardless of his two previous failures, insisted at Biarritz upon enlisting.

"The dog? what dog?" Guynemer had answered, not seeing an apologue in his father's words.

"The dog waiting at the door till somebody lets him in. His one thought is to get in while the people's minds are not concentrated on keeping him out. So he is sure to succeed in the end."

It is the same thing with our destiny, waiting till we open the door of our life. Vainly do we try to keep the door tightly shut against it: we cannot think of it all the time, and every now and then we fall into trustfulness, and thus its hour inevitably comes, and from the opening door it beckons to us. "What we call fatalism," M. Bergson says, "is only the revenge of nature on man's will when the mind puts too much strain upon the flesh or acts as if it did not exist. Orpheus, it is true, charmed the rivers, trees and rocks away from their places with his lyre, but the Maenades tore him to pieces in his turn."

We cannot say that the Guynemer who flew in Flanders was not the same Guynemer who had flown over the Somme, Lorraine or Aisne battlefields. Indeed, his mastery was increasing with each fresh encounter, and with his daring he cared little whether the enemy was gaining in numbers or inventing unsuspected tactics, His victories of August 17 and 20 showed him at his boldest best. Yet his comrades noticed that his nerves seemed overstrained. He was not content with flying oftener and longer than the others in quest of his game, but fretted if his Boche did not appear precisely when he wanted him. When an enemy did not turn up where he was expected, he made up his mind to seek him where he himself was not expected, and he became accustomed to scouting farther and farther away into dangerous zones. Was he tired of holding the door tight against destiny, or feeling sure that destiny could not look in? Did it not occur to him that his hour, whether near or not, was marked down?

Indeed, it is certain that the thought not only presented itself to him sometimes, but was familiar. "At our last meeting," writes his school-fellow of Stanislas days, Lieutenant Constantin, "I had been struck by his melancholy expression, and yet he had just been victorious for the forty-seventh time. 'I have been too lucky,' he said to me, 'and I feel as if I must pay for it.' 'Nonsense,' I replied, 'I am absolutely certain that nothing will happen to you.' He smiled as if he did not believe me, but I knew that he was haunted by the idea, and avoided everything that might uselessly consume a particle of his energy or disturb his sang-froid, which he intended to devote entirely to Boche hunting." [1]

[1] Unpublished notes by J. Constantin.

When had he ceased to think himself invincible? The reader no doubt remembers how he recovered from his wound at Verdun, and the shock it might have left, merely by flying and offering himself to the enemy's fire with the firm resolve not to return it. Eight times he had been brought down, and each time with full and prolonged consciousness of what was happening. On many occasions he had come back to camp with bullets in his machine, or in his combination. Yet these narrow escapes never reacted on his imagination, damped his spirit, or diminished his *furia*. But had he thought himself invincible? He believed in his star, no doubt, but he knew he was only a man. One of his most intimate friends, his rival in glory, the nearest to him since the loss of Dorme, the one who was the Oliver to this Roland, once received this confidence from Guynemer: "One of the fellows told me that when he starts up he only thinks of the fighting before him; he found that sufficiently absorbing; but I told him that when the men start my motor I always make a sign to the fellows standing around. 'Yes, I have seen it,' he answered; 'the handshake of the airman. It means *au revoir*.' But maybe it is farewell I am inwardly saying," Guynemer added, and laughed, for the boy in him was never far from the man.

Towards the end of July, while he was in Paris seeing to the repairs for his machine after bringing down his fiftieth enemy, he had gone to Compiègne for a short visit, His father, knowing his technical ability and his interest in all mechanical improvements, and on the other hand noticing a nervousness in his manner, dared for the first time to hint timidly and allusively at the possibility of his being useful in some other field.

"Couldn't you be of service with respect to making engines, etc.?"

But he was embarrassed by his son's look of questioning surprise. Every time Guynemer had used his father's influence in the army, it had been to bring himself nearer to danger.

"No man has the right to get away from the front as long as the war lasts," he said. "I see very well what you are thinking, but you know that self-sacrifice is never wasted. Don't let us talk any more about it . . ."

On Tuesday, August 28, Guynemer, having been obliged to come to Paris again for repairs to his airplane, went to Saint-Pierre de Chaillot. It was not exceptional for him to visit this old church; he loved to prepare himself there for his battle. One of the officiating priests has written since his death of "his faith and the transparency of his soul." [1] The Chaillot parishioners knew him well, but pretended not to notice him, and he thought himself one in a crowd. After seeing the priest in the confessional, he usually enjoyed another little chat in the sacristy, and although he was no man for long prayers and meditations, he expressed his thoughts on such occasions in heartfelt and serious language.

[1] *La Croix*, October 7, 1917, article by Pierre l'Ermite.

"My fate is sealed," he once said in his playful, authoritative way; "I cannot escape it." And remembering his not very far away Latin, he added: "*Hodie mihi, cras tibi ...*"

Early in September he made up his mind to go back to Flanders, although his airplane was not yet entirely repaired. The day before leaving he was standing at the door of the Hôtel Edouard VII when one of his schoolmates at the Collège Stanislas, Lieutenant Jacquemin, appeared. "He took me to his room," this officer relates, "and we talked for more than an hour about schooldays. I asked him whether he had some special dodge to be so successful." "None whatever," he said, "but you remember I took a prize for shooting at Stanislas. I shoot straight, and have absolute confidence in my machine." He showed me his numberless decorations, and was just as simple and full of good fellowship as he was at Stanislas. It was evident that his head had not been in the least turned by his success; he only talked more and enjoyed describing his fights. He told me, too, that in spite of opposition from airplane builders he had secured a long-contemplated improvement; and that he had had a special camera made for him with which he could photograph a machine as it fell. His parting words were: "I hope to fly to-morrow, but don't expect to see my name any more in the *communiqués*. That's all over: I have bagged my fifty Boches."

Were not these strange words, if indeed Guynemer attached any meaning to them? At all events,
they expressed his innermost longing, which was
to go on flying, even if he should fly for nothing.

Before reporting at Dunkirk, Guynemer spent
September 2, 3, and 4 with his people at Compiègne.
Never was he more fascinatingly affectionate, boyish, and bright than during those three days. But
he seemed agitated. "Let us make plans," he
said repeatedly, in spite of his old aversion to
castle-building. His plans that day were for the
amusement of his sisters. He reminded the younger,
Yvonne, that he had quarreled once with her. It
was at Biarritz, when he wanted her to make a
novena (nine days' special prayers) that he might
not be rejected by the recruiting board again; his
sister did not like to promise, and he had threatened
to sulk forever, which he had proceeded to do —
for five minutes.

His mother and sisters thought him more enchanting than ever, but his father felt that he was
overstrained, and realized that his almost morbid
notion of his duty as a chaser who could no longer
wait for his chance but wanted to force a victory,
was the result of fatigue. M. Guynemer no longer
hesitated to speak, adding that the period of rest
he advised was in the very interest of his son's
service. "You need strengthening; you have done
too much. If you should go on, you would be in
great danger of falling below yourself, or not really
being yourself."

"Father, war is nothing else. One must pull on, even if the rope should threaten to snap."

It was the first time that M. Guynemer had given undisguised advice, and he urged his point.

"Why not stop awhile? Your record is pretty good; you might form younger pilots, and in time go back to your squadron."

"Yes, and people would say that, hoping for no more distinctions, I have given up fighting."

"What does it matter? Let people talk, and when you reappear in better condition they will understand. You know I never gave you a word of advice which the whole world could not hear. I always helped you, and you always found the most disinterested approval here in your home. But you will admit that human strength has its limits."

"Yes," Georges interposed, "a limit which we must endeavor to leave behind. We have given nothing as long as we have not given everything."

M. Guynemer said no more. He felt that he had probed his son's soul to the depths, and his pride in his hero did not diminish his sorrow. When they parted he concealed his anguish, but he watched the boy, thinking he would never see him again. His wife and daughters, too, stood on the threshold oppressed by the same feelings, trying to suppress their anxiety and finding no words to veil it.

In the Iliad, Hector, after breaking into the Greek camp like a dark whirlwind unexpectedly sweeping the land, and which the gods alone could stop, returns to Troy and stopping at the Scæan

gates waits for Achilles, who he knows must be
wild to avenge Patroclus. Old Priam sees his son's
danger, and beseeches him not to seek his antago-
nist. Hecuba joins her tears to his supplications.
But tears and entreaties avail little, and Hector,
turning a deaf ear to his parents, walks out to
meet Achilles, as he thinks, but indeed to meet his
own fate.

On September 4, Guynemer was at the flying
field of Saint-Pol-sur-Mer near Dunkirk. His old
friend, Captain Heurtaux, so long Commander of
the Storks, was not there; he had been wounded
the day before by an explosive bullet, and the
English had picked up and evacuated him. Heurtaux possessed infinite tact, and had not infrequently succeeded in influencing the rebellious
Guynemer; but nobody was there to replace him.
September 5 was a day of extraordinary activity
for Guynemer. His magic airplane was still at the
works, where he had complained of not having
another in reserve; and not being able to wait for
it, he sent for his old machine and immediately
attacked a D. F. W. at close quarters, as usual;
but the Boche was saved by the jamming of both
of Guynemer's guns, and the aviator had to get
back to his landing-ground. Furious at this failure,
he promptly soared up again and attacked a chain
of five one-seated planes, hitting two, which however managed to protect each other and escape.
After two hours and a half, Guynemer went home
again, overhauled his guns, found a trigger out
of order, and for the third time went up again,

scouring the sky for two more hours, indignant to
see nothing but prudent Germans keeping far out
of his reach. So, he had flown five hours and a half
in that one day. What nerves could stand such a
strain? But Guynemer, seeking victory, cared
little for strain or nerves. Everything seemed to
go against him: Heurtaux away, his best machine
not available, his machine-guns out of order, and
Germans refusing his challenge. No wonder if he
fretted himself into increased irritation.

Guynemer liked Lieutenant Raymond, and every
now and then flew with him. This officer being on
leave, Guynemer on September 8 asked another
favorite comrade, *sous-lieutenant* Bozon-Verduraz,
to accompany him. The day was sullen, and a thick
fog soon parted the two aviators, who lost their
way and only managed to get clear of the fog when
Bozon-Verduraz was over Nieuport and Guynemer
over Ostend.

September 9 was a Sunday, and Guynemer over-
slept and had to be roused by a friend.

"Aren't you coming to mass?"

"Of course."

The two officers went to mass at Saint-Pol-sur-
Mer, and the weather having grown worse Guynemer did not fly; but instead of enjoying the
enforced rest, he resented it as a personal wrong.
Next day he flew three times, and was unlucky
again every time. On his first flight, on his two-gun
machine, he found that the water-pump control
did not work, and had to land on a Belgian aëro-

"GOING WEST"

drome, where he was welcomed and asked to sit
for his photograph. The picture shows a worried,
tense, disquieting countenance under the mask
ready to be pulled down. After frightening the
enemy so long, Guynemer was now frightening his
friends.

The photograph taken, Guynemer flew back to
camp. The best for him, under the circumstances,
would have been to wait. Was he not hourly to
hear that he might go to the Buc works for his
machine? And what was the use of flying on an
unsatisfactory airplane? But Guynemer was not
in Flanders to wait. He wanted his quarry, and he
wanted to set an example to and galvanize his men,
and even the infantry. So, Deullin being absent,
Guynemer borrowed his machine, and at last discovered a chain of German flyers, whom he attacked regardless of their number. But four bullets
hit his machine and one damaged the air-pump,
an accident which not only compelled him to land
but to return by motor to the aërodrome. Once
more, instead of listening to the whisper of wisdom,
he started, on Lieutenant Lagache's machine; and
this time the annoyance was the gasoline spurting
over the loose top of the carburetor. The oil caught
fire, and Guynemer had to give in, having failed
three times, and having been in the air five hours
and a half on unsatisfactory airplanes. No wonder if,
with the weather, the machines, and circumstances
generally against him, he felt tired and nervous.
He had never done so much with such poor results.
But his will, his will cannot accept what is forced

upon him, and we may be sure that he will not
acknowledge himself beaten.

III. THE LAST FLIGHT

On Tuesday, September 11, the weather was once
more uncertain. But morning fogs by the seaside
do not last, and the sun soon began to shine.
Guynemer had had a restless night after his
failures, and had brooded, as irritable people do,
over the very things that made him fretful. Chasing without his new airplane — the enchanting
machine which he had borne in his mind so many
months, as a woman bears her child, and which at
last he had felt soaring under him — was no pleasure. He missed it so much that the feeling became
an obsession, until he made up his mind to leave
for Buc before the day was over. Indeed, he would
have done so sooner had he not been haunted by
the idea that he must first bring down his Boche.
But since the Boche did not seem to be willing. . . .
Now he is resolved, and more calm; he will go to
Paris this very evening. He has only to while
away the time till the train is due. The prospect
in itself is quieting, and besides Major du Peuty,
one of the chiefs of Aviation at Headquarters, and
Major Brocard, recently appointed attaché to the
Minister of Aëronautics, were coming down by the
early train. They were sure to arrive at the camp
between nine and ten, and a conversation with
them could not but be instructive and illuminating;
so, better wait for them.

But, in spite of these tranquillizing thoughts, Guynemer was restless, and his face showed the sallow color which always foreboded his physical relapses. His mind was not really made up, and he would come and go, strolling from his tent to the sheds and from the sheds to his tent. He was not cross, only nervous. Suddenly he went back to the shed and examined his *Vieux-Charles*. Why, the machine was not so bad after all; the motor and guns had been repaired, and yesterday's accident was not likely to happen again. If so, why not fly? In the absence of Heurtaux, Guynemer was in command, and once more the necessity of setting a good example forced itself upon him. Several flyers had started on scouting work already; the fog was quickly lifting, the day would soon be resplendent, and the notion of duty too quickly dazzled him, like the sun. For duty had always been his motive power; he had always anticipated it, from the day when he was fighting to enlist at Biarritz to this 11th of September, 1917. It was neither the passion for glory nor the craze to be an aviator which had caused him to join, but his longing to be of use; and in the same way his last flights were made in obedience to his will to serve.

All at once he was really resolved. *Sous-lieutenant* Bozon-Verduraz was requested to accompany him, and the mechanicians wheeled the machines out. One of his comrades asked with assumed negligence: "Aren't you going to wait till Major du Peuty and Major Brocard arrive?" Guynemer's only answer was to wave towards the

sky then freeing itself from its veils of fog as he
himself was shaking off his hesitancy, and his
friend felt that he must not be urgent. Everybody
of late had noticed his nervousness, and Guynemer
knew it and resented it; tact was more necessary
than ever with him. Let it be remembered that he
was the pet, almost the spoiled child, of his service,
and that it had never been easy to approach him.

Meanwhile, the two majors, who had been met
at the station, were told of his nervous condition,
and hurried to speak to him. They expected to
reach the camp by nine o'clock, and would send
for him at once. But Guynemer and Bozon-
Verduraz had started at twenty-five minutes past
eight.

They had left the sea behind them, flying south-
east. They had reached the lines, following them
over Bixchoote and the Korteker Tavern which
the French troops had taken on July 31, over
the Bixchoote-Langemarck road, and finally over
Langemarck itself, captured by the British on
August 16. Trenches, sections of broken roads,
familiar to them from above, crossed and recrossed
each other under them, and they descried to the
north of Langemarck road the railway, or what
used to be the railway, between Ypres and Thour-
out and the Saint-Julien-Poelkapelle road. No
German patrol appeared above the French or
British lines, which Guynemer and his companion
lost sight of above the Maison Blanche, and they
followed on to the German lines over the faint
vestiges of Poelkapelle.

Guynemer's keen, long-practiced eye then saw a two-seated enemy airplane flying alone lower down than himself, and a signal was made to attract Bozon-Verduraz' notice. A fight was certain, and this fight was the one which Fate had long decided on.

The attack on a two-seater flying over its own lines, and consequently enjoying unrestricted freedom of movement, is known to be a ticklish affair, as the pilot can shoot through the propeller and the passenger in his turret rakes the whole field of vision with the exception of two angles, one in front, the other behind him under the fuselage and tail. Facing the enemy and shooting directly at him, whether upwards or downwards, was Guynemer's method; but it is not easy on account of the varying speeds of the two machines, and because the pilot as well as the passenger is sheltered by the engine. So it is best to get behind and a little lower than the tail of the enemy plane.

Guynemer had frequently used this maneuver, but he preferred a front attack, thinking that if he should fail he could easily resort to the other, either by turning or by a quick tail spin. So he tried to get between the sun and the enemy; but as ill-luck would have it, the sky clouded over, and Guynemer had to dive down to his opponent's level, so as to show him only the thin edges of the planes, hardly visible. But by this time the German had noticed him, and was endeavoring to get his range. Prudence advised zigzagging, for a cool-headed gunner has every chance of hitting a

straight-flying airplane; the enemy ought to be
made to shift his aim by quick tacking, and the
attack should be made from above with a full
volley, with the possibility of dodging back in case
the enemy is not brought down at once. But Guynemer, regardless of rules and stratagems, merely
fell on his enemy like a cannon ball. He might have
said, like Alexander refusing to take advantage of
the dark against Darius, that he did not want to
steal victory. He only counted on his lightning-like
manner of charging, which had won him so many
victories, and on his marksmanship. But he missed
the German, who proceeded to tail spin, and was
missed again by Bozon-Verduraz, who awaited him
below.

What ought Guynemer to do? Desist, no doubt.
But, having been imprudent in his direct attack,
he was imprudent again on his new tack, and his
usual obstinacy, made worse by irritation, coun-
seled him to a dangerous course. As he dived
lower and lower in hopes of being able to wheel
around and have another shot, Bozon-Verduraz
spied a chain of eight German one-seaters above the
British lines. It was agreed between him and his
chief that on such occasions he should offer himself
to the newcomers, allure, entice, and throw them
off the track, giving Guynemer time to achieve
his fifty-fourth success, after which he should fly
round again to where the fight was going on. He
had no anxiety about Guynemer, with whom he
had frequently attacked enemy squadrons of five,
six, or even ten or twelve one-seaters. The two-

seater might, no doubt, be more dangerous, and
Guynemer had recently seemed nervous and below
par; but in a fight his presence of mind, infallibility of movement, and quickness of eye were sure
to come back, and the two-seater could hardly
escape its doom.

The last image imprinted on the eyes of Bozon-
Verduraz was of Guynemer and the German
both spinning down, Guynemer in search of a
chance to shoot, the other hoping to be helped
from down below. Then Bozon-Verduraz had flown
in the direction of the eight one-seaters, and the
group had fallen apart, chasing him. In time the
eight machines became mere specks in the illim-
itable sky, and Bozon-Verduraz, seeing he had
achieved his object, flew back to where his chief
was no doubt waiting for him. But there was
nobody in the empty space. Could it be that the
German had escaped? With deadly anguish op-
pressing him, the airman descended nearer the
ground to get a closer view. Down below there was
nothing, no sign, none of the bustle which always
follows the falling of an airplane. Feeling reassured,
he climbed again and began to circle round and
round, expecting his comrade. Guynemer was
coming back, could not but come back, and the
cause of his delay was probably the excitement
of the chase. He was so reckless! Like Dorme —
who one fine morning in May, on the Aisne, went
out and was never heard of afterwards — he was
not afraid of traveling long distances over enemy
country. He must come back. It is impossible he

should not come back; he was beyond the reach of common accidents, invincible, immortal! This was a certitude, the very faith of the Storks, a tenet which never was questioned. The notion of Guynemer falling to a German seemed hardly short of sacrilege.

So Bozon-Verduraz waited on, making up his mind to wait as long as necessary. But an hour passed, and nobody appeared. Then the airman broadened his circles and searched farther out, without, however, swerving from the rallying-point. He searched the air like Nisus the forest in his quest of Euryalus, and his mind began to misgive him.

After two hours he was still waiting, alone, noticing with dismay that his oil was running low. One more circle! How slack the engine sounded to him! One more circle! Now it was impossible to wait any more: he must go back alone.

On landing, his first word was to ask about Guynemer.

"Not back yet!"

Bozon-Verduraz knew it. He knew that Guynemer had been taken away from him.

The telephone and the wireless sent their appeals around, airplanes started on anxious cruises. Hour followed hour, and evening came, one of those late summer evenings during which the horizon wears the tints of flowers; the shadows deepened, and no news came of Guynemer. From neighboring camps French, British, or Belgian comrades arrived, anxious for news. Everywhere the latest birds had come home, and one hardly dared ask the airmen any question.

But the daily routine had to be dispatched, as if there were no mourning in the camp. All the young men there were used to death, and to sporting with it; they did not like to show their sorrow; but it was deep in them, sullen and fierce.

At dinner a heavy melancholy weighed upon them. Guynemer's seat was empty, and no one dreamed of taking it. One officer tried to dispel the cloud by suggesting hypotheses. Guynemer was lucky, had always been; probably he was alive, a prisoner.

Guynemer a prisoner!... He had said one day with a laugh, "The Boches will never get me alive," but his laugh was terrible. No, Guynemer could not have been taken prisoner. Where was he, then?

On the squadron log, *sous-lieutenant* Bozon-Verduraz wrote that evening as follows:

Tuesday, September 11, 1917. Patrolled. Captain Guynemer started at 8.25 with *sous-lieutenant* Bozon-Verduraz. Found missing after an engagement with a biplane above Poelkapelle (Belgium).

That was all.

IV. THE VIGIL

Before Guynemer, other knights of the air, other aces, had been reported missing or had perished — some like Captain Le Cour Grandmaison or Captain Auger in our lines, others like Sergeant Sauvage and *sous-lieutenant* Dorme in the enemy's. In fact, he would be the thirteenth

on the list if the title of ace is reserved for aviators to whom the controlling board has given its
visé for five undoubted victories. These were the
names:

Captain Le Cour Grandmaison	5	victories
Sergeant Hauss	5	"
sous-lieutenant Delorme . . .	5	"
sous-lieutenant Pégoud	6	"
sous-lieutenant Languedoc . .	7	"
Captain Auger	7	"
Captain Doumer	7	"
sous-lieutenant Rochefort . . .	7	"
Sergeant Sauvage	8	"
Captain Matton	9	"
Adjutant Lenoir	11	"
sous-lieutenant Dorme	23	"

Would Guynemer's friends now have to add:
Captain Guynemer, 53? Nobody dared to do so,
yet nobody now dared hope.

A poet of genius, who even before the war had
been an aviator, Gabriele d'Annunzio, has described in his novel, *Forse che sì forse che no*, the
friendship of two young men, Paolo Tarsis and
Giulio Cambasio, whose mutual affection, arising
from a similar longing to conquer the sky, has
grown in the perils they dare together. If this book
had been written later, war would have intensified
its meaning. Instead of dying in a fight, Cambasio
is killed in a contest for altitude between Bergamo
and the Lake of Garda. As Achilles watched beside
the dead body of Patroclus, so Tarsis would not
leave to another the guarding of his lost friend:

"In tearless grief Paolo Tarsis kept vigil through the short summer night. So it had broken asunder the richest bough on the tree of his life; the most generous part of himself ruined. For him the beauty of war had diminished, now that he was no longer to see, burning in those dead eyes, the fervor of effort, the security of confidence, the rapidity of resolution. He was no longer to taste the two purest joys of a manly heart: steadiness of eye in attack, and the pride of watching over a beloved peer."

For him the beauty of war had diminished.... War already so long, so exhausting and cruel, and laden with sorrow! Will war appear in its horrid nakedness, now that those who invested it with glory disappear, now, above all, when the king of these heroes, the dazzling young man whose luminous task was known to the whole army, is no more? Is not his loss the loss of something akin to life? For a Guynemer is like the nation's flag: if the soldiers' eyes miss the waving colors, they may wander to the wretchedness of daily routine, and morbidly feed on blood and death. This is what the loss of a Guynemer might mean.

But can a Guynemer be quite lost?

SAINT-POL-SUR-MER, *September*, 1917
(From the author's diary)

Visited the Storks Escadrille.

The flying field occupies a vast space, for it is common to the French and the British. A dam protecting the landing-ground screens it from the sea. But from the second floor of a little house which the bombs have left standing, you can see its moving expanse of a delicate, I might say timid blue, dotted with home-coming boats. The evening is placid and fine, with a reddish haze blurring the horizon.

Opposite the sheds, with their swelling canvas walls, a row of airplanes is standing before being rolled in for the night. The mechanicians feel them with careful hands, examining the engines, propellers, and wings. The pilots are standing around, still in their leather suits, their helmets in their hands. In brief sentences they sum up their day's experiences.

Mechanically I look among them for the one whom the eye invariably sought first. I recalled his slight figure, his amber complexion, and dark, wonderful eyes, and his quick descriptive gestures. I remembered his ringing, boyish laugh, as he said:

"And then, '*couic*' . . ."

He was life itself. He got out of his seat panting but radiant, quivering, as it were, like the bowstring when it has sent its shaft, and full of the sacred drunkenness of a young god.

Ten days had passed since his disappearance. Nothing more was known than on that eleventh of September when Bozon-Verduraz came back alone. German prisoners belonging to aviation had not heard that he was reported missing. Yet it was inconceivable that such a piece of news should not have been circulated; and, in fact, yesterday a

message dropped by a German airplane on the
British lines, concerning several English aviators
killed or in hospital, was completed by a note
saying that Captain Guynemer had been brought
down at Poelkapelle on September 10, at 8 A.M.
But could this message be credited? Both the day
and hour it stated were wrong. On September 10
at 8 A.M. Guynemer was alive, and even the next
day he had not left the camp at the hour mentioned. An English newspaper had announced his
disappearance, and perhaps the enemy was merely
using the information. The mystery remained un-
solved.

As we were discussing these particulars, the
last airplanes were landing, one after another, and
Guynemer's companions offered their reasons for
hoping, or rather believing; but none seemed convinced by his own arguments. Their inner conviction must be that their young chief is dead;
and besides, what is death, what is life, to devoting
one's all to France?

Captain d'Harcourt had succeeded Major Brocard pro tem as commandant of the unit. He was
a very slim, very elegant young man, with the
grace and courtesy of the *ancien régime* which his
name evoked, and the perfection of his manners
and gentleness seemed to lend convincing power
to all he said. Guynemer being missing and
Heurtaux wounded, the Storks were now commanded by Lieutenant Raymond. He belonged
to the cavalry, a tall, thin man, with the sharp
face and heroic bearing of Don Quixote, a kindly

man with a roughness of manner and a quick,
picturesque way of expressing himself. Deullin
was there, too, one of Guynemer's oldest and most
devoted friends. Last of all descended from the
high regions *sous-lieutenant* Bozon-Verduraz, a
rather heavy man with a serious face, and more
maturity than belonged to his years, an unassum-
ing young man with a hatred for exaggeration and
a deep respect for the truth.

Once more he went through every detail of the
fatal day for me, each particular anticipating the
dread issue. But in spite of this narrative, full of the
idea of death, I could not think of Guynemer as
dead and lying somewhere under the ground held
by the enemy. It was impossible for me not to
conjure up Guynemer alive and even full of life,
Guynemer chasing the enemy with strained terrible eyes, Guynemer of the superhuman will, the
Guynemer who never gave up, — in short, a
Guynemer whom death could not vanquish.

A wonderful atmosphere men breathe here, for it
relieves death of its horror. One officer, Raymond,
I think, said in a careless manner:

"Guynemer's fate will be ours, of course."

Somebody protested: "The country needs men
like you."

To which Deullin answered: "Why does it?
There will be others after us, and the life we
lead. . . ."

But Captain d'Harcourt broke in gaily: "Come
on; dinner's ready — and with this bright moon
and clear sky we are sure to get bombed."

Bombed, indeed, we were, and pretty severely, but in convenient time, for we had just drunk our coffee. A few minutes before, the practiced ear of one of us had caught the sound of the *bimoulins*, the bi-motor German airplanes, and soon they were near. We gained the sheltering trench. But the night was so entrancingly pure, with the moon riding like an airship in the deep space, that it seemed to promise peace and invited us to enjoy the spectacle. We climbed upon the parapet and listened to the breathing of the sea, accompanying with its bass the music of the motors. There were still a few straggling reddish vapors over the luminous landscape, and the stars seemed dim. But other stars took their place, those of the French *Voisins* returning from some bombing expedition, their lights dotting the sky like a moving constellation, while at intervals a rocket shot from one or the other who was anxious not to miss the landing-ground. Over Dunkirk, eight or ten searchlights stretched out their long white arms, thrusting and raking to and fro after the enemy machines. Suddenly one of these appeared, dazzled by the revealing light, as a moth in the circle of a lamp; our batteries began firing, and we could see the quick sparks of their shells all around it. Flashing bullets, too, drew zebra-like stripes across the sky, and with the cannonade and the rumbling of the airplanes we heard the lament òf the Dunkirk sirens announcing the dreaded arrival of the huge 380 shells upon the town, where here and there fires broke out. Mean-

while the German airplanes got rid of their bombs
all around us, and we could feel the ground tremble.

The Storks looked on with the indifference of
habit, thinking of their beds and awaiting the end.
One of them, a weather prophet, said:

"It will be a good day to-morrow; we can start
early."

As I spun towards Dunkirk in the motor, these
young men and their speeches were in my mind,
and I seemed to hear them speaking of their absent
companion without any depression, with hardly
any sorrow. They thought of him when they were
successful, referred to him as a model, found an
incentive in his memory, — that was all. Their
grief over his loss was virile and invigorating.

After watching his friend's body through the
night, the hero of d'Annunzio goes to the aërodrome where the next trials for altitude are to
take place. He cannot think of robbing the dead
man of his victory. As he rises into the upper
regions of the air he feels a soothing influence and
an increase of power: the dead man himself pilots
his machine, wields the controls, and helps him
higher, ever higher up in divine intoxication.

In the same way the warlike power of Guynemer's companions is not diminished. Guynemer is
still with them, accompanying each one, and in-
stilling into them the passionate longing to do
more and more for France.

V. THE LEGEND

In seaside graveyards, the stone crosses above the empty tombs say only, after the name, "Lost at sea." I remember also seeing in the churchyards of the Vale of Chamonix similar inscriptions: "Lost on Mont-Blanc." As the mountains and the sea sometimes refuse to give up their victims, so the air seems to have kept Guynemer.

"He was neither seen nor heard as he fell," M. Henri Lavedan wrote at the beginning of October; "his body and his machine were never found. Where has he gone? By what wings did he manage thus to glide into immortality? Nobody knows: nothing is known. He ascended and never came back, that is all. Perhaps our descendants will say: "He flew so high that he could not come down again." [1]

I remember a strange line read in some Miscellany in my youth and never forgotten, though the rest of the poem has vanished from memory:

Un jet d'eau qui montait n'est pas redescendu.

Does this not embody the upspringing force of Guynemer's brilliant youth?

Throughout France some sort of miracle was expected: Guynemer must reappear — if a prisoner he must escape, if dead he must come to life. His father said he would go on believing even to the extreme limits of improbability. The journalist who signs his letters from the front to *Le Temps*

[1] *L'Illustration*, October 6, 1917.

with the pseudonym d'Entraygues recalled a passage from Balzac in which some peasants at work on a haystack call to the postman on the road: "What's the news?" "Nothing, no news. Oh! I beg your pardon, people say that Napoleon has died at St. Helena." Work stops at once, and the peasants look at one another in silence. But one fellow standing on the rick says: "Napoleon dead! psha! it's plain those people don't know him!" The journalist added that he heard a speech of the same kind in the bush-region of Aveyron. A passenger on the motor-bus read in a newspaper the news of Guynemer's death; everybody seemed dismayed. The chauffeur alone smiled skeptically as he examined the spark plugs of his engine. When he had done, he pulled down the hood, put away his spectacles, carefully wiped his dirty hands on a cloth still dirtier, and planting himself in front of the passenger said: "Very well. *I* tell you that the man who is to down Guynemer is still an apprentice. Do you understand? . . ."

The credulity of the poor people of France with regard to their hero was most touching. When the death of Guynemer had to be admitted, there was deep mourning, from Paris to the remote villages where news travels slowly, but is long pondered upon. Guynemer had been brought down from a height of 700 meters, northeast of Poelkapelle cemetery, in the Ypres sector. A German noncommissioned officer and two soldiers had immediately gone to where the machine was lying. One of the wings of the machine was broken;

the airman had been shot through the head, and
his leg and shoulder had been broken in the fall;
but his face was untouched, and he had been
identified at once by the photograph on his pilot's
diploma. A military funeral had been given to him.
Nevertheless, it seemed as if Guynemer's fate
still remained somewhat obscure. The German
War Office published a list of French machines
fallen in the German lines, with the official in-
dications by which they had been recognized. Now,
the number of the *Vieux-Charles* did not appear
on any of these lists, although having only one
wing broken the number ought to have been
plainly visible. Who were the noncommissioned
officer and the two soldiers? Finally, on October 4,
1917, the British took Poelkapelle, but the enemy
counter-attacked, and there was furious fighting.
On the 9th the village was completely occupied
by the British, and they searched for Guynemer's
grave. No trace of it could be found in either
the military or the village graveyard.

In fact, the Germans had to acknowledge in an
official document that both the body and the airplane of Guynemer had disappeared. On November 8, 1917, the German Foreign Office replied as
follows to a question asked by the Spanish Ambas-
sador:

Captain Guynemer fell in the course of an air fight
on September 11 at ten A.M. close to the honor graveyard No. 2 south of Poelkapelle. A surgeon found that
he had been shot through the head, and that the fore-
finger of his left hand had been shot off by a bullet.

The body could neither be buried nor removed, as the place had been since the previous day under constant and heavy fire, and during the following days it was impossible to approach it. The sector authorities communicate that the shelling had plowed up the entire district, and that no trace could be found on September 12 of either the body or the machine. Fresh inquiries, which were made in order to answer the question of the Spanish Embassy, were also fruitless, as the place where Captain Guynemer fell is now in the possession of the British.

The German airmen express their regret at having been unable to render the last honors to a valiant enemy.

It should be added that investigation in this case was only made with the greatest difficulty, as the enemy was constantly attacking, fresh troops were frequently brought in or relieved, and eye witnesses had either been killed or wounded, or transferred. Our troops being continually engaged have not been in a position to give the aforesaid information sooner.

So there had been no military funeral, and Guynemer had accepted nothing from his enemies, not even a wooden cross. The battle he had so often fought in the air had continued around his body; the Allied guns had kept the Germans away from it. So nobody can say where lies what was left of Guynemer: and no hand had touched him. Dead though he was, he escaped. He who was life and movement itself, could not accept the immobility of the tomb.

German applause, like that with which the Greeks welcomed the dead body of Hector, did not fail to welcome Guynemer's end. At the end of three weeks a coarse and discourteous paean was sung in the *Woche.* In its issue of October 6, this paper devoted to Guynemer, under the title "Most Successful French Aviator Killed," an article whose lying cowardice is enough to disgrace a newspaper, and which ought to be preserved to shame it. A reproduction of Guynemer's diploma was given with the article, which ran as follows:

Captain Guynemer enjoyed high reputation in the French army, as he professed having brought down more than fifty airplanes, but many of these were proved to have got back to their camps, though damaged it is true. The French, in order to make all verification on our side impossible, have given up stating, in the past few months, the place or date of their so-called victories. Certain French aviators, taken prisoner by our troops, have described his method thus: sometimes, when in command of his squadron, he left it to his men to attack, and when he had ascertained which of his opponents was the weakest, he attacked that one in turn. Sometimes he would fly alone at very great altitudes, for hours, above his own lines, and when he saw one of our machines separated from the others would pounce upon it unawares. If his first onset failed, he would desist at once, not liking fights of long duration, in the course of which real gallantry must be displayed.[1]

[1] Der Erfolgreichste Französische Kamfflieger Gefallen. Kapitän Guynemer genoss grossen Ruhm im französischen Heere, da er 5o Flugzeuge abgeschossen haben wollte. Von diesen ist jedoch nachgewiesenermassen eine grosse Zahl, wenn auch beschädigt, in ihre Flughäfen zurück-

This is the filth the German paper was not ashamed to print. Repulsive though it is, I must analyze some of its details. An enemy's abuse reveals his own character. So this German denied the fifty-three victories of Guynemer, all controlled, and with such severity that in his case, as in that of Dorme, he was not credited with fully a third of his distant triumphs, too far away to be officially recognized; so this German also vilified Guynemer's fighting methods, Guynemer the foolhardy, the wildly, madly foolhardy, whose machines and clothes were everlastingly riddled with bullets, who fought at such close quarters that he was constantly in danger of collisions — this Guynemer the German journalist makes out to be a prudent and timid airman, shirking fight and making use of his comrades. What sort of story had the German who brought him down told? Was it not obvious that if Guynemer had engaged him at 4000 meters, and had been killed at 700, that he

gekert. Um deutscherseits eine Nachprüfung unmöglich zu machen, wurden in den letzten Monaten Ort und Datum seiner angeblichen Luftsiege nicht mehr angegeben. Ueber seine Kampfmethode haben gefangene französische Flieger berichtet: Entweder liess er, als Geschwaderführer fliegend, seine Kameraden zuerst angreifen un stürzle sich dann erst auf den schwächsten Gegner; oder er flog stundenlang in grössten Höhe, allein hinter der französischen Front und stürzte sich von oben herab überraschend auf einzeln fliegende deutsche Beobachtungsflugzeuge. Hatte Guynemer beim ersten Verstoss keinen Erfolg, so brach er das Gefecht sofort ab; auf den länger dauernden, wahrhaft muterprobenden Kurvenkampf liess er sich nicht gern ein. — Extract from the *Woche* of October 6, 1917.

must have prolonged the struggle, and prolonged it above the enemy's lines? Finally, the German journalist had the unutterable meanness and infamy to saddle on imprisoned French aviators this slander of their comrade, insinuated rather than boldly expressed. After all, this document is invaluable, and ought to be framed and preserved. How Guynemer would have laughed over it, and how youthfully ringing and honest the laugh would have sounded! Villiers de l'Isle Adam, remembering the Hegelian philosophy, once wrote: "The man who insults you only insults the idea he has formed of you, that is to say, himself."

As a whole army (the Sixth) marched on May 25 towards that hill of the Aisne valley where Guynemer had brought down four German machines, and acclaimed his triumph, so the whole French nation would take part in mourning him.

At the funeral service held at Saint Antony's Compiègne, the Bishop of Beauvais, Monseigneur Le Senne, spoke, taking for his text the Psalm in which David laments the death of Saul and his sons slain *on the summits*, and says that this calamity must be kept secret lest the Philistines and their daughters should rejoice over it. This service was attended by General Débeney, staff major-general, representing the generalissimo, and by all the surviving members of the Storks Escadrille, with their former chief, Major Brocard. His successor, Captain Heurtaux, whose unexpected appearance startled the congregation — he seemed so pale and thin on his crutches — had left the hospital for this ceremony, and looked so ill that people were surprised that he had the strength to stand.

A few hours before the service took place, Major Garibaldi, sent by General Anthoine, commander of the army to which Guynemer belonged, had brought to the Guynemer family the twenty-sixth citation of their hero, the famous document which all French schoolboys have since learned by heart and which was as follows:

Fallen on the field of honor on September 11, 1917. A legendary hero, fallen from the very zenith of victory after three years' hard and continuous fighting. He will be considered the most perfect embodiment of the national qualities for his indomitable energy and perseverance and his exalted gallantry. Full of invincible belief in victory, he has bequeathed to the French soldier an imperishable memory which must add to his self-sacrificing spirit and will surely give rise to the noblest emulation.

On the motion of M. Lasies, in a session which reminded us of the great days of August, 1914, the Chamber decided on October 19 that the name of Captain Guynemer should be graven on the walls of the Panthéon. Two letters, to follow below, were read by M. Lasies, to whom they had been written. One came from Lieutenant Raymond, temporary commandant of the Storks, and was as follows:

Having the honor to command Escadrille 3 in the absence of Captain Heurtaux, still wounded in hospital, I am anxious to thank you, in the name of the few surviving Storks, for what you are doing for the memory of Guynemer.

He was our friend as well as our chief and teacher, our pride and our flag, and his loss will be felt more than any that has thinned our ranks so far.

Please be sure that our courage has not been laid low with him; our revenge will be merciless and victorious.

May Guynemer's noble soul remember us fighting our aërial battles, that we may keep alight the flame he bequeathed to us.

RAYMOND

Commanding Escadrille 3.

The other letter came from Major Brocard:

MY DEAR COMRADE:

I am profoundly moved to hear of the thought you have had of giving the highest consecration to Guynemer's memory by a ceremony at the Panthéon.

It had occurred to all of us that only the lofty dome of the Panthéon was large enough for such wings.

The poor boy fell in the fullness of triumph, with his face towards the enemy. A few days before he had sworn to me that the Germans should never take him alive. His heroic death is not more glorious than that of the gunner defending his gun, the infantryman rushing out of his trench, or even that of the poor soldier perishing in the bogs. But Guynemer was known to all. There were few who had not seen him in the sky, whether blue or cloudy, bearing on his frail linen wings some of their own faith, their own dreams, and all that their souls could hold of trust and hope.

It was for them all, whether infantrymen or gunners or pioneers, that he fought with the bitter hatred he felt for the invader, with his youthful daring and the joys of his triumphs. He knew that the battle would end fatally for him, no doubt, but knowing also that his war-bird was the instrument of saving thousands of lives, and seeing that his example called forth the noblest imitation, he remained true to his idea of self-sacrifice which he had formed a long time before, and which he saw develop with perfect calm.

Full of modesty as a soldier, but fully conscious of the greatness of his duties, he possessed the national qualities of endurance, perseverance, indifference to danger, and to these he added a most generous heart.

During his short life he had not time enough to learn bitterness, or suffering, or disillusionment.

He passed straight from the school where he was learning the history of France to where he himself could add another page to it. He went to the war driven by a mysterious power which I respect as death or genius ought to be respected.

He was a powerful thought living in a body so delicate that I, who lived so close beside him, knew it would some day be slain by the thought.

The poor boy! Other boys from every French school wrote to him every day. He was their legendary ideal, and they felt all his emotions, sharing his joys as well as his dangers. To them he was the living copy of the heroes whose exploits they read in their books. His name is constantly on their lips, for they love him as they have been taught to love the purest glories of France.

Monsieur le député, gain admittance for him to the Panthéon, where he has already been placed by the mothers and children of France. There his protecting wings will not be out of place, for under that dome where sleep those who gave us our France, they will be the symbol of those who have defended her for us.

MAJOR BROCARD.

These letters roused the enthusiasm of the Chamber, and the following resolution was passed by acclamation:

The government shall have an inscription placed in the Panthéon to perpetuate the memory of Captain Guynemer, the symbol of France's highest aspirations.

On November 5 the foregoing letters were solemnly read aloud in every school, and Guynemer was presented as an example to all French schoolboys.

The army then prepared to celebrate Guynemer as a leader, and in default of any place suitable for such a ceremony they selected the camp of Saint-Pol-sur-Mer, whence Guynemer had started on his last flight. On November 30 General Anthoine, commanding the First Army, before leaving the Flemish British sector where he had so brilliantly assisted in the success, decided to associate his men with the glorification of Guynemer.

The ceremony took place at ten in the morning. A raw breeze was blowing off the sea, whose violence the dam, raised to protect the landing-ground, was not sufficient to break. In front of the battalion which had been sent to render the military honors, waved the colors of the twenty regiments that had fought in the Flemish battles, glorious flags bearing the marks of war, some of them almost in rags. To the left, in front of the airmen, two slight figures were visible, one in black, one in horizon blue: Captain Heurtaux still on his crutches, the

other *sous-lieutenant* Fonck. The former was to
be made an officer, the latter a chevalier in the
Legion of Honor. Heurtaux, a fair-haired, delicate,
almost girlish young man, but so phenomenally
self-possessed in danger, had been, as we have
said, our Roland's Oliver, his companion of old
days, his rival and his confidant. Fonck, whom I
called Aymerillot because of his smallness, his
boyish simplicity and his daring, the hope of the
morrow and already a glorious soldier, had perhaps avenged Guynemer's death already. For
Lieutenant Weissman, according to the *Kölnische
Zeitung*, had boasted in a letter to his people of
having brought down the most famous French
aviator. "Don't be afraid on my account," he
added, "I shall never meet such a dangerous
enemy again." Now, on September 3o Fonck had
shot this Lieutenant Weissman through the head
as the latter was piloting a Rumpler machine
above the French lines.

While the band was playing the *Marseillaise*,
accompanied by the roaring of the gale and of the
sea, as well as of the airplanes circling above,
General Anthoine stepped out in front of the row
of flags. His powerful frame seemed to suggest the
cuirass of the knights of old, as, silhouetted against
the cloudy sky, he towered above the two diminu-
tive aviators near whom he was standing. The
band stopped playing, and the general spoke, his
voice rising and falling in the wind, and swelling
to a higher pitch when the elements were too rebellious. He was speaking almost on the spot where

Guynemer had departed from the soil of his own country on his final flight.

"I have not summoned you," he said, "to pay Guynemer the last homage he has a right to from the First Army, over a coffin or a grave. No trace could be found in Poelcapelle of his mortal remains, as if the heavens, jealous of their hero, had not consented to return to earth what seems to belong to it by right, and as if Guynemer had disappeared in empyrean glory through a miraculous assumption. Therefore we shall omit, on this spot from which he soared into Infinity, the sorrowful rites generally concluding the lives of mortals, and shall merely proclaim the immortality of the Knight of the Air, without fear or reproach.

"Men come and go, but France remains. All who fall for her bequeath to her their own glory, and her splendor is made up of their worth. Happy is he who enriches the commonwealth by the complete gift of himself. Happy then the child of France whose superhuman destiny we are celebrating! Glory be to him in the heavens where he reigned supreme, and glory be to him on the earth, in our soldiers' hearts and in these flags, sacred emblems of honor and of the worship of France!

"Ye flags of the second aëronautical unit and of the First Army, you keep in the mystery of your folds the memory of virtue, devotion, and sacrifice of every kind, to hand down to future generations the treasures of our national traditions!

"Flags, the souls of our heroes live in you, and

when your fluttering silk is heard, it is indeed
their voice bidding us go from the same dangers
to the same triumphs!

"Flags, keep the soul of Guynemer forever. Let
it raise up and multiply heroes in his likeness!
Let it exalt to resolution the hearts of neophytes
eager to avenge the martyr by imitating his lofty
example, and let it give them power to revive
the prowess of this legendary hero!

"For the only homage he expects from his companions is the continuation of his work.

"In the brief moment during which dying men
see, as in a vision, the whole past and the whole
future, if Guynemer knew a comfort it was the
certainty that his comrades would successfully
complete what he had begun.

"You, his friends and rivals, I know well; I
know that, like Guynemer, you can be trusted, that
you meet bravely the formidable task he has
bequeathed to you, and that you will fulfil the
hopes which France had reposed in him.

"It is to confirm this certitude in presence of our
flags, brought to witness it, that I am glad to con-
fer on two of his companions, two of our bravest
fighters, distinctions which are at the same time
a reward for the past and an earnest of future
glory."

Then the general gave the accolade and embraced Heurtaux, now less dependent on his
crutches, and Fonck, suddenly grown taller, children of glory, both of them, and still pale from
the emotion caused by the evocation of their

friend's glory. He pinned the badges on their coats.
After this he added, in a lull of the conflicting elements: Ⅼⅈ

"Let us raise our hearts in respectful and grateful admiration for the hero whom the First Army
can never forget, of whom it was so proud, and
whose memory will always live in History.

"Dead though he be, a man like Guynemer
guides us, if we know how to follow him, along the
triumphal way which, over ruins, tombs, and
sacrifices, leads to victory the good and the
strong."

Of itself, thanks to this religious conclusion of
the general's ode, the ceremony had assumed a sort
of sacred character, and the word which concludes
prayers, the Amen of the officiating priest, naturally came to our lips while the general saluted with
his sword the invisible spirit of the hero, and the
blasts of the bugles rose above the gale and the
sea.

VI. IN THE PANTHÉON

In the Panthéon crypt, destined, as the inscription says, for the burial of great men, the name of
Guynemer will be graven on a marble slab ce-
mented in the wall. The proper inscription for this
slab will be the young soldier's last citation:

FALLEN ON THE FIELD OF HONOR ON SEP-
TEMBER 11, 1917. A LEGENDARY HERO, FALLEN
FROM THE VERY ZENITH OF VICTORY AFTER
THREE YEARS' HARD AND CONTINUOUS FIGHT-
ING. HE WILL BE CONSIDERED THE MOST PER-
FECT EMBODIMENT OF THE NATIONAL QUALITIES
FOR HIS INDOMITABLE ENERGY AND PERSE-
VERANCE AND HIS EXALTED GALLANTRY. FULL
OF INVINCIBLE BELIEF IN VICTORY, HE HAS
BEQUEATHED TO THE FRENCH SOLDIER AN
IMPERISHABLE MEMORY WHICH MUST ADD TO
HIS SELF-SACRIFICING SPIRIT AND WILL SURELY
GIVE RISE TO THE NOBLEST EMULATION.

"To deserve such a citation and die!" exclaimed
a young officer after reading it.

In his poem, *Le Vol de la Marseillaise*, Rostand
shows us the twelve Victories seated at the Invalides around the tomb of the Emperor rising to
welcome their sister, the Victory of the Marne.
At the Panthéon, in the crypt where they rest,
Marshal Lannes and General Marceau, Lazare
Carnot, the organizer of victory, and Captain La
Tour d'Auvergne will rise in their turn on this
young man's entrance. Victor Hugo, who is there
too, will recognize at once one of the knights in
his *Légende des Siècles*, and Berthelot will look upon
his coming as an evidence of the fervor of youth
for France as well as for science. But of them all,
Marceau, his elder brother, killed at twenty-seven,
will be the most welcoming.

Traveling in the Rhine Valley some ten or
twelve years ago, I made a pilgrimage to Marceau's

tomb, outside Coblenz, just above the Moselle. In a little wood stands a black marble pyramid with the following inscription in worn-out gilt letters:

Here lieth Marceau, a soldier at sixteen, a general at twenty-two, who died fighting for his country the last day of the year IV of the Republic. Whoever you may be, friend or foe, respect the ashes of this hero.

The French prisoners who died in 1870–71 at the camp of Petersberg have been buried, on the same spot. Marceau was not older than these soldiers, who died without fame or glory, when his brief and wonderful career came to an end. Without knowing it, the Germans had completed the hero's mausoleum by laying these remains around it; for it is proper that beside the chief should be represented the anonymous multitude without whom there would be no chiefs.

In 1889 the remains of Marceau were transferred to the Panthéon in Paris, and the Coblenz monument now commemorates only his name. It will be the same with Guynemer, whose remains will never be found, as if the earth had refused to engulf them; they will never be brought back, amidst the acclamations of the people, to the mount once dedicated to Saint Genevieve. But his legendary life was fitly crowned by the mystery of such a death.

One of the frescoes of Puvis de Chavannes in the Panthéon, the last to the left, represents an old woman leaning over a stone terrace and gazing

at the town beneath her with its moonlit roofs and
its surrounding plain, looking bluish in the night.
The city is asleep, but the holy woman watches
and prays. She stands tall and upright as a lily.
Her lamp, which is seen at the entrance of her
house, is one long stem illuminated by the flame.
She, too, is like this lamp. Her emaciated body
would be nothing without her ardent face. Her
serenity can only come from work well done and
confidence in the future. Lutetia, represented in
this picture by Genevieve, is not anxious; yet she
listens as if she might hear once more the threat-
ening approach of Attila. It is because she knows
that the barbarians may come back again, and
can only be stopped by invincible faith.

As long as France keeps her belief, she is secure.
The life and death of a Guynemer are an act of
faith in immortal France.

ENVOI

The *ballades* of olden times used to conclude
with an *envoi* addressed to some powerful person
and invariably beginning with King, Queen, Prince
or Princess. But the poet was occasionally at a loss,
for, as Theodore de Banville observes in his *Petit
traité de Poésie Française*, "everybody has not a
prince handy to whom to dedicate his *ballade.*"

Guynemer's biography is of such a nature that
it must seem like a poem: why not, then, conclude
it with an *envoi?* I have no difficulty in finding a
Prince, for I shall select him from among the

French schoolboys. There is a little Paul Bailly, not quite twelve years old, from Bouclans, a village in Franche-Comté, who wrote a beautiful theme on Guynemer: he shall be my Prince. And through him I shall address all the French schoolboys or girls, in all the French towns and villages.

Little Prince, I have no doubt that you love arithmetic, and I will give you accurate figures which will satisfy your taste. You will like to know that Guynemer flew for 665 hours and 55 seconds in all, which I added up from his flying notebooks: his last flight is not recorded in them, because it never stopped.

As for the number of fights in which he was engaged, that is difficult to ascertain. Guynemer himself did not seem anxious to be sure about it. But it must be more than 600, and might well be 700 or 800. Your Guynemer, our Guynemer, will never be surpassed: not because he forgot to hand over to his successors, rivals, and avengers the sacred flame which in France can never go out, but because genius is an exceptional privilege, and because the present methods of fighting in the air are not in favor of single combats but engage whole units.

You will also love to hear about Guynemer as an inventor, and the creator of a magic airplane. Some day this airplane will be exhibited; and perhaps some of your little friends have already seen at the Invalides the machine in which Guynemer brought down nineteen German airplanes. On November 1, 1917, thousands of Parisians visited it; and it was strewn with magnificent bunches of chrysanthemums, to which many people added clusters of violets.

In Guynemer the technician and the marksman equaled and perhaps surpassed the pilot. Captain Galliot, who is a specialist, has called him "the thinker-fighter," thereby emphasizing that his excellence as a gunner arose from meditation and preparation. The same officer adds that "accuracy was Guynemer's characteristic; he never shot at random as others occasionally do, but always took long and careful aim. Perfect weapons and perfect mastery of them were dogmas with him. His marksmanship, the result of perseverance and intelligence, multiplied tenfold the capacity of his machine-gun, and accounts for his overwhelming superiority." [1]

But when you have realized the technical superiority of our Guynemer, you will have yet to learn one thing, one great thing, the essential thing. You have heard that Guynemer's frame was not robust; that he was delicate, and the military boards refused him several times as unfit. Yet no aviator ever showed more endurance than he did, even when developments made long cruising necessary in altitudes of 6000 or 7000 meters. There have been pilots as quickwitted and gunners as accurate as Guynemer, but there has never been anybody who equaled him in the flashlike rapidity of his attack, or for doggedness in keeping up a fight. We must conclude that he had a special gift,

[1] *Guerre aérienne*, October 18, 1917.

and this gift — his own genius — must be ultimately reduced to his decision, that is, his will-
power. His will, to the very end, was far above
his physical strength. There are two great dates in
his short life: November 21, 1914, when he joined
the army, and September 11, 1917, when he left
camp for his last flight. Neither a passion for
aviation nor thirst for glory had any part in his
action on those two dates. Will-power in itself is
sometimes dangerous, enviable though it be, and
must be wisely directed. Now, Guynemer regulated his will by one great object, which was to
serve, to serve his country, even unto death.

Finally, do not place Guynemer apart from his
comrades: even in his grave, even in the region
where there is no grave, he would resent it. I hope
you will learn by heart the names of the French
aces, at any rate those names which I am going
to give you, whatever may become of those who
bear them: [1]

sous-lieutenant Nungesser	30 airplanes brought down	
Captain Heurtaux	21 "	"
Lieutenant Deullin. . . .	17 "	"
Lieutenant Pinsard . . .	16 "	"
sous-lieutenant Madon . .	16 "	"
sous-lieutenant Chaput . .	12 "	"
Adjutant Jailler	12 "	"
sous-lieutenant Ortoli . . .	11 "	"
sous-lieutenant Tarascon .	11 "	"
Chief Adjutant Fonck . .	11 "	"
sous-lieutenant Lufbery . .	10 "	"

[1] List made September 11, 1917.

These names will become more and more glorious — some have already done so — and others will be added to the list which you will learn also. But however tenacious your memory may be, you will never remember, nobody will ever remember, the thousands of names we ought to save from oblivion, the names of those whose patience, courage, and sufferings have saved the soil of France. The fame of one man is nothing unless it represent the obscure deeds of the anonymous multitude. The name of Guynemer ought to sum up the sacrifice of all French youth — infantrymen, gunners, pioneers, troopers, or flyers — who have given their lives for us, as we hear the infinite murmur of the ocean in one beautiful shell.

The enthusiasm and patience, the efforts and sacrifices, of the generations which came before you, little boy, were necessary to save you, to save your country, to save the world, born of light and born unto light, from the darkness of dread oppression. Germany has chosen to rob war of all that, slowly and tentatively, the nations had given to it of respect for treaties, pity for the weak and defenseless, and of honor generally. She has poisoned it as she poisons her gases. This is what we should never forget. Not only has Germany forced this war upon the world, but she has made it systematically cruel and terrifying, and in so doing she has sown the seeds of horrified rebellion against anything that is German. Parisian boys of your own age will tell you that during their sleep German squadrons used to fly over their city dropping bombs at random upon it. And to what purpose? None, beyond useless murder. This is the kind of war which Germany has waged from the first, gradually compelling her opponents to adopt the same methods. But while this loathsome work was being done, our airplanes, piloted by soldiers not much older than you, cruised like moving stars above the city of Genevieve, threatened now with unheard-of invasion from on high.

Little boy, do not forget that this war, blending all classes, has also blended in a new crucible all the capacities of our country. They are now turned against the aggressor, but they will have to be used in time for union, love, and peace. *Omne regnum divisum contra se desolabitur; et omnis civitas vel domus divisa contra se non stabit.* You can read this easy Latin, but if necessary your teacher or village priest will help you. The house, the city, the nation ought not to be divided. The enemy would have done us too much evil if he had not brought about the reconciliation of all Frenchmen. You, little boy, will have to wipe away the blood from the bleeding face of France, to heal her wounds, and secure for her the revival she will urgently need. She will come out of the formidable contest respected and admired, but oh, how weary! Love her with pious love, and let the life of Guynemer inspire you with the resolve to serve in daily life, as he served, even unto death.

December, 1917, to *January*, 1918.

APPENDIX

APPENDIX

GENEALOGY OF GEORGES GUYNEMER

In *Huon de Bordeaux*, a *chanson de geste* with fairy and romantic elements, Huon leaves for Babylon on a mission confided to him by the Emperor, which he was told to fulfil with the aid of the dwarf sorcerer, Oberon. At the château of Dunôtre, in Palestine, where he must destroy a giant, he meets a young girl of great beauty named Sébile, who guides him through the palace. As he is astonished to hear her speak French, she replies: "I was born in France, and I felt pity for you because I saw the cross you wear." "In what part of France?" "In the town of Saint-Omer," replied Sébile; "I am the daughter of Count Guinemer." Her father had lately come on a pilgrimage to the Holy Sepulchre, bringing her with him. A tempest had cast them on shore near the town of the giant, who had killed her father and kept her prisoner. "For more than seven years," she added, "I have not been to mass." Naturally Huon kills the giant, and delivers the daughter of Count Guinemer.

In an article by the learned M. Longnon on *L'Elément historique de Huon de Bordeaux*,[1] a note is given on the name of Guinemer:

[1] *Romania*, 1879, p. 4.

"In *Huon de Bordeaux*," writes M. Longnon, "the author of the *Prologue des Lorrains* makes Guinemer the son of Saint Bertin, second Abbot of Sithieu, an abbey which took the name of this blessed man and was the foundation of the city of Saint-Omer, which the poem of *Huon de Bordeaux* makes the birthplace of Count Guinemer's daughter. It is possible that this Guinemer was borrowed by our *trouveres* from some ancient Walloon tradition; for his name, which in Latin is Winemarus, appears to have occurred chiefly in those countries forming part, from the ninth to the twelfth century, of the County of Flanders. The chartulary of Saint Vertin alone introduces us to: 1st, a deacon named Winidmarus, who in 723 wrote a deed of sale at Saint-Omer itself (Guérard, p. 50); 2d, a knight of the County of Flanders, Winemarus, who assassinated the Archbishop of Rheims, Foulques, who was then Abbot of Saint-Bertin (Guérard, p. 135); 3d, Winemarus, a vassal of the Abbey, mentioned in an act dated 1075 (*ib.*, p. 195); 4th, Winemarus, Lord of Gand, witness to a charter of Count Baudouin VII in 1114 (*ib.*, p. 255). The personage in *Huon de Bordeaux* might also be connected with Guimer, Lord of Saint-Omer, who appears in the beginning of *Ogier le Danios*, if the form, Guimer, did not seem rather to derive from Withmarus."[1]

[1] With this note may be connected the following page of the Wauters, a chronological table of Charters and printed Acts, Vol. II, p. 16, 1103: "Baldéric, Bishop of the Tournaisiens and the Noyonnais, confirms the cession of the

Leaving the *chansons de geste*, Guinemer re-appears in the history of the Crusades. Count Baudouin of Flanders and his knights, while making war in the Holy Land (1097), see a vessel approaching, more than three miles from the city of Tarsus. They wait on the shore, and the vessel casts anchor. "Whence do you come?" is always the first question asked in like circumstances. "From Flanders, from Holland, and from Fries-land." They were repentant pirates, who after having combed the seas had come to do penance by a pilgrimage to Jerusalem. The Christian war-riors joyously welcome these sailors whose help will be useful to them. Their chief is a Guinemer, not from Saint-Omer but Boulogne. He recognizes in Count Baudouin his liege lord, leaves his ship and decides to remain with the crusaders. "*Moult estait riche de ce mauvais gaeng.*" The whilom pirate contributes his ill-gotten gains to the crusade.[1]

In another chapter of the *Histoire des Croisades*, this Guinemer besieged Lalische, which "is a most noble and ancient city situated on the border of

tithe and patronage of Templeuve, which was made to the Abbey of Saint-Martin de Tournai by two knights of that town, Arnoul and Guinemer, and by the canon Géric. *Actum Tornaci, anno domenice incarnationis M.C. III, regnante rege Philippo, episcopante domo Baldrico pontifice.* Extracts for use in the ecclesiastic history of Belgium, 2d year, p. 10."

[1] *Receuil des Historiens des Croisades*, Western Historians, Volume I, Book III and XXIII, p. 145: *Comment Guinemerz et il Galiot s'accompaignierent avec Baudouin.*

the sea; it was the only city in Syria over which
the Emperor of Constantinople was ruler." Lalische or Laodicea in Syria, *Laodicea ad mare* —
now called Latakia — was an ancient Roman
colony under Septimus Severus, and was founded
on the ruins of the ancient Ramitha by Seleucus
Nicator, who called it Laodicea in honor of his
mother Laodice. Guinemer, who expected to take
the city by force, was in his turn assaulted and
taken prisoner by the garrison. Baudouin, with
threats, demanded him back and rescued him;
but esteeming him a better seaman than a combatant on the land, he invited him to return to
his ship, take command of his fleet, and navigate
within sight of the coast, which the former pirate
"very willingly did."

A catalogue of the Deeds of Henri I, King of
France (1031-1060)[1] mentions in this same period
a Guinemer, Lord of Lillers, who had solicited the
approval of the king for the construction of a
church in his château, to be dedicated to Notre-
Dame and Saint-Omer. The royal approval was
given in 1043, completing the authorization of
Baudouin, Count of Flanders, and of Dreu,
Bishop of Thérouanne at the request of Pope
Gregory VI, to whom the builder had gone in
person to ask consent for his enterprise. Was this
Guinemer, like the pirate of Jerusalem, doing
penance for some wrong? Thus we find two Guine-
mers in the eleventh century, one in Palestine,

[1] *Catalogue des actes d'Henri I, Roi de France* (1031-1060),
by Frédéric Soehnée, archivist at the National Archives.

the other in Italy. About this same period the
family probably left Flanders to settle in Brittany,
where they remained until the Revolution. The
corsair of Boulogne became a ship-builder at Saint-
Malo, having his own reasons for changing parishes.
The Flemish tradition then gives place to that of
Brittany, which is authenticated by documents.
One Olivier Guinemer gave a receipt in 1306 to the
executors of Duke Jean II de Bretagne. He held
a fief under Saint-Sauveur de Dinan, "on which the
duke had settled tenants contrary to agreements."
The executors, to liquidate the estate, had to pay
immense sums for "indemnification, restitution
and damages," and took care to "take receipts
from all those to whom their commission obliged
them to distribute money."[1] The Treaty of Gué-
rande (April 11, 1365), which ended the war for
the Breton succession and gave the Duchy to
Jean de Montfort, though under the suzerainty
of the King of France, is signed by thirty Breton
knights, among whom is a Geoffroy Guinemer. A
Mathelin Guinemer, squire, is mentioned in an
act received at Bourges in 1418; while in 1464, an
Yvon Guynemer, man-at-arms, is promoted to full
pay, and he already spells his name with a y.

It is somewhat difficult to trace the history of
this lesser provincial nobility, engaged sometimes
in petty wars, sometimes in the cultivation of

---

[1] *Histoire de Bretagne,* by Dom Lobineau (1707), Vol. I,
p. 293. *Recherches sur la chevalerie du duché de Bretagne,*
by A. de Couffon de Kerdellech, Vol. II (Nantes, Vincent
Forest and Emile Grimaud, Printers and Publishers).

their domains. In a book glorifying the humble service of ancient French society, *Gentilshommes Campagnards*, M. Pierre de Vaissiére has shown how this race of rural proprietors lived in the closest contact with French agriculture, counseling and defending the peasant, clearing and cultivating their land, and maintaining their families by its produce. In his *Mémoires*, the famous Rétif de la Bretonne paints in the most picturesque manner the patriarchal and authoritative manners of his grandfather who, by virtue of his own unquestioned authority prevented his descendant from leaving his native village and establishing in Paris. Paris was already exercising its fascination and uprooting the youth of the time. The Court of Versailles had already weakened the social authority of families still attached to their lands.

Made in the USA
San Bernardino, CA
15 September 2018